Beyond The Window

Beyond The Window

A FAITH COMMUNITY IN
AMERICA'S HEARTLAND

———

Scott Killgore

Foreword by Dr. Richard L. Hamm

Beyond the Window
Printed by CreateSpace

Scripture quotations are from the ESV® Bible (The Holy Bible, English Standard Version®),
copyright © 2001 by Crossway, a publishing ministry of Good News Publishers. Used by
permission. All rights reserved.
Copyright © 2017 Scott Killgore
ISBN-13: 9781973777977
ISBN-10: 1973777975

Library of Congress Control Number: 2017912914
CreateSpace Independent Publishing Platform
North Charleston, South Carolina

To the people who gather at Twenty-Seventh Street and Mitchell Avenue. They *are* Wyatt Park Christian Church, and even now they are writing new chapters in this continuing story.

Contents

Foreword

——

I WAS HONORED WHEN PASTOR Scott Killgore, friend and colleague, invited me to prepare a foreword for this delightful telling of the story of Wyatt Park Christian Church (Disciples of Christ). This congregation has been an essential part of the spiritual, moral, and cultural life of St. Joseph, Missouri, and far beyond, for more than a century. It has reached inward to the people of St. Joe and outward across the globe through mission efforts on many continents.

Wyatt Park began as part of a movement that was sweeping across the United States in the nineteenth century, making the gospel of Jesus Christ accessible to all kinds of people without the barriers often created by complicated denominational particularities. The Stone-Campbell Movement reshaped the American church in significant ways, especially in its preaching, teaching, and practicing of the essential unity of all Christians. That legacy continues today as the ecumenical character of the church is taken for granted in most quarters and denominations that used to be in opposition to one another now share in mission together.

Wyatt Park Christian Church was also part of an unselfish desire of established congregations to start new congregations in the interest of providing new places and opportunities for all the people to come to know, love, and serve Jesus Christ. First Christian Church even commissioned some of its own members to help get Wyatt Park started. That mission impulse is expressed in Jesus's teaching: "Whoever seeks to save his life will lose it, but whoever loses his life for my sake will find it" (Matt. 16:25). It is as the church "gives itself away" in mission that it finds its life. Mission is, in fact, the lifeblood of the church. This has been demonstrated again and again by Wyatt Park's generous and self-giving commitment to mission. I was deeply touched, for example, by the story of the "conscience fund" found in chapter 2. It is part of your very DNA. From "nesting" a new Hispanic congregation to investing in missions around the world, Wyatt Park has demonstrated wonderful faithfulness to the gospel call to both share the faith and meet the basic needs of human beings wherever they live.

This congregation has been served by a number of outstanding ministers, many of whom it is or has been my pleasure and privilege to know: Lawrence Bash (a mentor of mine during my sojourn as a young minister in Kansas City), Wally Brown, Gene Mockabee, and, of course, Scott Killgore. Wyatt Park has also contributed excellent ministers to the whole body of Disciples including my friend Kyle Maxwell. You have also been served by steadfast lay leaders who have served not only this congregation but the whole Christian Church (Disciples of Christ) with faithfulness and dedication.

To my mind, the same mission-minded commitment and uncomplicated presentation of the gospel that has always defined Wyatt Park makes it a congregation that is as relevant today as it once was in the nineteenth and twentieth centuries. Your ongoing desire to maintain flexibility in season after season of cultural change, coupled with your sincere desire to *be something beautiful for God* and to continue to reach those who need to know about the love of God made known through Jesus Christ, makes you a continuing vital witness. Thanks be to God!

May your journey in faith and faithfulness continue for another century and beyond. The whole world and whole church of Jesus Christ need more congregations like Wyatt Park Christian Church (Disciples of Christ). May you be blessed in each new season of mission and ministry to come.

The Rev. Dr. Richard L. Hamm
Former General Minister and President (1993–2003)
Christian Church (Disciples of Christ) in the
United States and Canada
Indianapolis, Indiana
Summer 2017

Acknowledgments

I BEGIN BY THANKING THE people who, for more than a century, have kept the records of Wyatt Park Christian Church safe and stored in an orderly way. I thank the volunteers who spent about three years gathering photos, news clippings, and so forth and organizing them into historical scrapbooks (see chapter 5 for more on their work).

I thank our daughter Rebecca "Becky" Meneely, who was a *very* thorough editor. She carefully read the draft of each chapter and returned those drafts with many notes in red. She has made this a better book. I thank Kara (Davison) Klontz, who was like a daughter to us as she grew up at Wyatt Park. Her graphic-design skills grace the cover of this book. I thank Dr. Richard Hamm for writing the Foreword and even more for his friendship, counsel, and leadership. I am grateful to Dr. Gene Mockabee, a tremendous colleague and mentor during my first nine-plus years at Wyatt Park and a dear friend yet today.

I am grateful to Mary Ellen Dedman, who went home to Jesus many years ago. In 1968 she published *A Spire to God*, which told the story of the congregation in which I grew up, First Christian Church, Plattsburg, Missouri. She set the bar high in terms of congregational histories, and she helped inspire me to try writing the story of Wyatt Park Christian Church.

I thank my wife, Deirdra (Deedie), who put up with five years of evening and weekend research and writing and nearly a year of having one room of our home decorated with many boxes of historical materials. Through it all she was supportive and encouraging. I am blessed.

Above all, I give thanks to God. He gave me life and eternal life in Christ. He called me to ministry and then called me to an amazing community of faith that has been my church home for twenty-one years and counting.

Introduction

BEYOND THE WINDOW IS A title that speaks to the most iconic physical component of Wyatt Park Christian Church. The *Creation Window* is a forty-foot high work of art to the glory of God, and it dominates the south end of the sanctuary that has been a St. Joseph landmark since 1957. Passersby likely see the sanctuary and wonder what goes on inside, "beyond the window." Church members and visitors gather in the sanctuary each week to connect with one another, worship God, grow in their walks with Christ, and be spiritually fed for another week of life outside, "beyond the window." And, by virtue of its design, the *Creation Window* points beyond itself, "beyond the window," to God who created heaven and earth, has given us life, and through Jesus Christ offers eternal life to all who will receive it.

This is the story of a faith community located in the middle of America's heartland. In some ways, this could be the story of any midsized Christian congregation, but it is also the story of a particular congregation in a particular place at a particular time, so its story is also unique.

I gave myself this project five years ago because of my love of history and for this congregation and also because of a desire to see if I could follow the lead of Luke the Gospel writer and "write an orderly account for you" (Luke 1:3). Over four years, countless evening and weekend hours were spent poring over large quantities of historical material that had been stored safely and was well organized. It took almost another year to write this story, which may best be thought of as a "congregational portrait." That image comes from one of my seminary history professors who also became a friend, Dr. Anthony Dunnavant. Sadly, cancer claimed his life a few years ago, but he taught me a lot, and he wrote a book about undertakings such as this. He concluded his book with this statement:

> The finished product of a congregational historian's work will be, at best, a portrait. It will be one artist's view. It will be impressionistic rather than photographically realistic, because the historian will have chosen only some colors, only some lines, from the mass of information that he or she has encountered. It will be a static view because that is the nature of the canvas of the written word, while we know that the congregation's story is, in fact, dynamic and continually changing.[1]

Regarding method, I have chosen to take a historian's approach, so I draw almost entirely from the congregation's written record. Thankfully, the written record is vast and includes meeting minutes, newsletters, and files of all types and thicknesses. For the most part, I have written in the third person, but in those few sections where I am discussed in some way, I have chosen to write in the first person.

A note about footnotes: *please read them.* Granted, most of the footnotes simply indicate where a particular piece of information was found, but several footnotes contain information that was worthy of inclusion in the book but did not seem to fit into the main body of text.

What you hold is a labor of love—love for a very special community of faith that I have been privileged to serve for twenty-one years and love for the one in whose name this faith community exists, our Savior and Lord Jesus Christ. May God bless you as you read this story, this portrait, and may He bless you as you love and serve Him at Wyatt Park—or wherever life's journey may take you.

St. Joseph, Missouri
August 2017

---

1 Anthony Dunnavant, *Backgrounds for Congregational Portraits* (Nashville, TN: The Disciples of Christ Historical Society, 1994), 116.

CHAPTER 1

The Beginnings

——

*...and you will be my witnesses in Jerusalem and in all Judea
and Samaria, and to the ends of the earth. (Acts 1:8)*

ST. JOSEPH WAS BOOMING IN 1888, but not for reasons that one might think of when considering the city in the nineteenth century. The Pony Express had gone bankrupt seventeen years earlier, replaced by telegraph lines and railroads. Families and gold seekers hoping for riches, or simply a better life, had long since completed their wagon journeys west, thousands of them having passed through St. Joseph where they stocked up on provisions before entering the Kansas Territory.

What drove St. Joseph's bustling economy in 1888? Wholesaling and meat-packing. The Civil War was over, and people were again moving west, settling on farms and in communities that grew rapidly all across Missouri, Kansas, and beyond. Those settlers needed supplies, and St. Joseph businessmen met that need, wholesaling everything from groceries to hardware and from dry goods to lumber. The meat-packing industry, already established for several years, grew dramatically when the St. Joseph Stockyards opened for business in December 1887.

Jobs were plentiful, and people came to St. Joseph in large numbers so that by 1888, the city's population reached an estimated seventy thousand people. With so many people, the city extended far beyond the original area that planner Frederick Smith had laid out in 1843 for founder Joseph Robidoux.

One of the rapidly growing areas of St. Joseph in 1888 was south and east of downtown and several blocks east of the landmark Patee House Hotel. That fast-growing area came to be known as Wyatt Park.

There was never a public park by that name. Rather, Wyatt Park designated a subdivision named for an Atchison County, Missouri, farmer. Archibald Wyatt lived near Rock Port, where he was also a banker and political leader. He served in the Missouri House and later as a state senator. Although he never lived in St. Joseph, Wyatt had an office in the city, and he was likely a major investor in the Wyatt Park Land Company, which developed the subdivision. In January 1889, the *St. Joseph Gazette* described Wyatt Park as a "beautiful suburb."[1] More than a year earlier, that "beautiful suburb" had gotten the attention of Marshall Monroe (M. M.) Goode, the pastor at First Christian Church in downtown St. Joseph.

The Christian Church

As the nineteenth century began, religious reform was underway in North America and Europe. In the thick of it were three men whose faith and efforts led to the formation of a new group of churches (denomination), one of the few such groups actually born in North America. Ironically, they did not want to start a new denomination at all. They wanted denominations to disappear.

Thomas Campbell and his son, Alexander, were born in Ireland. Thomas was a teacher, but after a few years in the classroom, he decided to enter the ministry. He served Presbyterian churches in Ireland before immigrating to America in 1807, settling in southwestern Pennsylvania near the town of Washington. He sent for his family, and they attempted the journey in 1808, but a shipwreck prevented their travel, and they stayed in Glasgow, Scotland, for almost a year. That proved to be a formative time for the young Alexander Campbell who seized the opportunity to study at the University of Glasgow. Unbeknown to both him and his father, Alexander and Thomas were each

---

1 I am grateful to Bob Slater of St. Joseph for researching the origin of the name Wyatt Park.

becoming more reform minded, and that was quickly evident when the family reunited in 1809.

Both men were disturbed by what they witnessed in the Presbyterian Church. They believed the church had lost sight of the gospel and was instead focused on preserving and strengthening an institution, and they saw denominations as being unnecessarily divisive. They left the Presbyterian Church and united with Baptists for a while but eventually ended up on their own with the beginnings of a movement that became known as the Disciples of Christ.

Their efforts to reform the church of Jesus Christ quickly attracted followers and even congregations. Growth of the Disciples movement was aided by the fact that Alexander Campbell gained notoriety as a writer and speaker on matters of faith and the church. As he became well known, he also came to assume the leading position within the Disciples movement. Campbell published a monthly journal beginning in 1823. He published it as *The Christian Baptist* until 1830 when the name was changed to *The Millennial Harbinger*. Campbell made a name for himself as a preacher and debater, and he attracted more and more followers. There was no television or Internet in the nineteenth century, so people read journals, often more than one. Consequently, some of Campbell's followers noted similarities between the ideas of the Disciples of Christ and those of a reform movement centered in Kentucky. That reform movement's journal was *The Christian Messenger* and its publisher was Barton Stone.

Born in Port Tobacco, Maryland, Stone was the only one of the three religious reformers born in America. As a young man, he entered Guilford Academy in North Carolina intending to study law, but during his second year, he changed direction and decided instead to preach the gospel. He first served small Presbyterian churches in eastern North Carolina, but eventually he was called to serve as the pastor of Presbyterian congregations in Cane Ridge and Concord, Kentucky, and it was there that his reform views were solidified.

Stone's views were strikingly similar to those of Alexander Campbell, and as more people read the publications of both men, there was a growing call for Stone and Campbell to work together. The union of their reform movements did not happen quickly or easily, but it was made formal on January 1, 1832, during a meeting in Lexington, Kentucky.

Campbell and Stone did not agree on everything. They had heated debates in their journals, both of which continued to be published after the union. One point of disagreement centered on what to call their unified reform movement. Stone argued that the term "Christian" was adequate and complete, so his followers generally referred to themselves as Christians, and their churches were known simply as Christian Churches. Campbell believed that the term "Disciples" was better because it more effectively pointed to the calling of the faithful to follow Jesus. The two never agreed on the name, and the result is today's bulky denominational label, Christian Church (Disciples of Christ). Despite their disagreements, the union was made possible by core principles that they shared.

Most historians of the Campbell-Stone reform movement readily acknowledge three core principles, with two additional principles suggested by some:

1. *Individual freedom to study and interpret scripture.* While they believed preaching is an important element of worship, they also believed that ultimately it is up to each believer to study and interpret the Bible. Not surprisingly, their advocacy of individual freedom was received very well in the rapidly expanding American frontier.

2. *Restoration of New Testament Christianity.* They promoted a return to "simple New Testament" Christianity, believing that the New Testament tells us what we need to know about church structure, offices, practices, and so forth. They pointed to the book of Acts in particular.

3. *Unity of believers.* This is what Jesus prayed for (John 17:20–23). Campbell and Stone longed for the day when denominational differences would disappear and the Body of Christ would speak with a unified voice.

4. *Evangelization.* The late Disciples historian Anthony Dunnavant includes this as a core principle, and it is made possible by a combination of the first three. Believers who study and interpret the Bible

and return to "simple New Testament" Christianity will be unified in their proclamation of the gospel, and the result will be the evangelization and transformation of the world.[2]

5. *Eschatological.* This is a fancy word having to do with the end times, and Disciples historian Mark Toulouse convincingly suggests this as one of the core principles shared by the founders. He notes the name of Campbell's newspaper, *The Millennial Harbinger*, suggesting that a good interpretation of the eschatological principle is "God with us." Campbell believed that God has been a living actor in history and yet is also present and active today. Just as God was encountered by human beings in the past, he can be, and is, encountered by human beings today. Before history there was God. After history there will be God. Within history there is God. It all centers on Christ, and Christians stand in the midst of time that is being redeemed.[3]

As the population of the young nation migrated west, so did the reform movement of Barton Stone and Alexander Campbell. In Missouri, the first congregation linked to the reformers was in Howard County near the town of Fayette. It was organized in 1816. By 1840, congregations dotted the state, and in 1845, the first Campbell-Stone congregation in St. Joseph started to form. The congregation known today as First Christian Church began with meetings in the homes of church members in 1845. Those meetings continued until 1850, when the church was formally organized and began worshiping downtown. Seven pastors served the congregation over the next 30 years, and in 1881, M.M. Goode began his ministry at First Christian Church. He had a heart for evangelism, which resulted in many people coming to faith in Jesus Christ, and also the formation of new churches in a rapidly growing city.

---

2 Lexington Theological Seminary, class notes, "Church History 532—History of the Christian Church (Disciples of Christ)," Anthony Dunnavant, instructor, February 3, 1994.

3 Mark Toulouse, *Joined in Discipleship: The Shaping of Contemporary Disciples Identity* (St. Louis, MO: Chalice Press, 1997), 127–28.

Rev. M.M. Goode

Marshall Monroe Goode was born in 1838 about fifty miles northeast of St. Louis in McCoupin County, Illinois. His father died when he was five years old, and he then went to live with his maternal grandfather. Farming was the family's means of support, which meant hard work, and as was generally the case in the expanding nation in the early nineteenth century, educational opportunities were limited. Rev. Goode loved music and became skilled with the violin, so he was frequently called upon to play for dances and other social gatherings.

M.M. Goode was twenty-two years old when he became a Christian, a decision that changed the course of his life. His religious fervor and natural talent for public speaking quickly led him to conclude that he was to spend his life preaching the gospel. He began preaching in small churches, mostly near his home in Illinois. In 1860, he married Mary Russell, and they had two daughters. The Goodes were together for seventeen years until Mary's death in 1877. After her death, he continued his work as a pastor while also raising their two daughters (he married Florence Clark in 1885).

Rev. Goode's brother-in-law, John Corwine, was also a pastor. He filled the pulpit for a short time in St. Joseph at First Christian Church, and through that family connection, Goode was invited to preach at First Christian in January 1881. Afterward, the congregation asked him to become its pastor. He served First Christian for the next seventeen years and then served for twelve years as the pastor of Wyatt Park Christian Church. By the end of his career, Rev. Goode had spent more than sixty years in ministry and nearly forty-two years in St. Joseph.[4]

---

4 *Pieces of Our Lives*, published by First Christian Church, St. Joseph, Missouri, for that congregation's sesquicentennial, 1995: 10. Additional information is drawn from multiple articles and newspaper clippings including the *St. Joseph News-Press*: March 23, 1906, and April 10, 1906; *The Christian Standard*, April 7, 1906; and other articles from the same period that are bound together, but for which publication dates are not available. The bound documents are stored with meeting minutes from Wyatt Park's earliest years.

Membership increased significantly during Rev. Goode's tenure at First Christian Church, but there was another type of growth during his ministry—the number of churches in St. Joseph. Under his leadership, First Christian Church started Sunday-School classes in different parts of the city. In time, several of those classes were organized into congregations. Woodson Chapel Christian Church began as a Sunday-School class on the north side of the city. Mitchell Park Christian Church began in the same way on south Twelfth Street. Rev. Goode was also instrumental in the beginnings of King Hill Christian Church and a congregation on Frederick Avenue (known today as Central Christian Church). In March 1888, a committee at First Christian Church started to search for possible locations for a Sunday-School class in the new Wyatt Park addition.

A Sunday-School class began during the summer of 1888 in a vacant building at the corner of Twenty-Seventh and Olive. Shortly thereafter, it was organized as a congregation, Wyatt Park Christian Church. Illustrative of his unselfish nature, Rev. Goode went before the congregation of First Christian Church and encouraged some members to transfer to the newly organized church. Although it is not known how many actually did so, it is likely that at least some of the thirty-two charter members of Wyatt Park Christian Church came from the downtown congregation.

Rev. Goode also encouraged the congregation of First Christian Church to help raise funds to construct a building for Wyatt Park Christian Church. The response was positive. Financial gifts were received and a lot was donated at the northwest corner of Twenty-Seventh and Olive. The donation was conditional: the lot had to be used to erect a church building. Ground was broken for the new building on February 1, 1889, and the building was dedicated to the Lord the following summer.[5]

---

5 The story of Wyatt Park Christian Church's beginnings has been published in short form multiple times. For purposes of this chapter, the primary resource was a short history of the church published on the occasion of the congregation's fiftieth anniversary. The document is dated June 12, 1938.

CHAPTER 2

The Gathering Place

––––

Unless the Lord builds the house, those who
build it labor in vain. (Ps. 127:1)

"CHURCH" IS TRANSLATED FROM A Greek word, *ecclesia*, and in the most general sense, it refers to a gathering of people. In the New Testament, the word refers to an assembly of Christians gathered for worship. Most of the time in the New Testament, *ecclesia* is used to refer to a specific group of people, such as the Corinthians, Philippians, and so forth. Jesus used the word to speak of his followers gathered in any city or village (Matt. 18:17) and in reference to all who worship and honor God and Christ wherever they may be (Matt. 16:18).[1] "Church" is *not* used in the New Testament to refer to a building.

Granted, believers must gather to worship *somewhere,* but even if a congregation's worship location (i.e., a building) is destroyed, the church will still exist because it consists of the people, not wood, bricks, and mortar. Thankfully, the buildings that have housed Wyatt Park Christian Church since 1888 have never been destroyed. Replaced and renovated, yes, but never destroyed.

Wyatt Park Christian Church may be its people, but the buildings have played a major role in the congregation's story. A church building is a tool that

––––

1 Thayer's Greek Lexicon, *Strongs NT 1577: ecclesia* (Electronic Database: Biblesoft, Inc., 2002, 2003, 2006, 2011).

provides a place to gather for worship, education, and fellowship and from which church members go out into the world to live and serve in Jesus's name.

"A Cozy Home-Like Church"

The donor's condition was met: a white, wood-frame church building was constructed on the donated lot at Twenty-Seventh and Olive. It cost $2,500 to construct, and nearly half of that total came from members of First Christian Church.[2] Nothing is known about the floor plan, but a small 1889 folder described it as "A Cozy, Home-Like Church." The building had a basement, and in the summer of 1889, not long after it was first opened, the newly forming Wyatt Park Baptist Church was invited to use two of the basement rooms. A remodeling program was undertaken soon after M.M. Goode became the congregation's pastor in 1898, and the remodeled building was rededicated on November 24, 1902.[3]

Building maintenance was important then, as today, but there were differences. The cost of goods and services is an example. It was noted in June 1914

---

2 Information concerning building cost and funding sources is found on a typed sheet filed with the Board Minutes, March 1939.

3 "Church History," Mrs. F. G. Innis, Wyatt Park Christian Church, *Programme of Dedicatory Services*, October 7–14, 1928.

that "the church has been painted and repaired at a cost of about $144."[4] The bill was forwarded to the Ladies Aid Society for payment. Three months later, the board learned that the church building had been insured for $2,500 for three years at a cost of $75.[5] In 1915, the board dealt with an issue churches face today—parking. However, times were different, as revealed by the notation: "Question of the hitching post also referred to the committee" (Building and Grounds Committee).[6]

As the city grew and the Wyatt Park neighborhood continued to develop, Wyatt Park Christian Church also grew. No attendance or membership records from the early years have been found, but it was reported to the board in January 1918 that 191 pledges had been received in the "Every Member Canvass (congregation-wide pledge campaign)."[7] It was noted at the next meeting that fifty-one people still had not been canvassed.[8] Regardless of exact numbers, growth was significant enough to prompt the pastor, John Love, to recommend that the congregation undertake a "program of construction." His proposal was received favorably, but it would be another twenty-one months before there would be additional action. In November 1919, the board agreed to begin a three-year fund-raising campaign for a new building.[9]

At the end of that three-year period, the board received a report from the committee investigating whether to build a new church or remodel the existing facility. Several options were discussed, but no decision was made, at least not then.[10] Eventually, the decision was made to construct a new building. In June 1923, it was "Moved and seconded that the chairman appoint a committee to select a location for the new church. Carried."[11]

---

4 Board minutes, June 8, 1914.
5 Board minutes, September 7, 1914.
6 Board minutes, November 1, 1915.
7 Board minutes, January 7, 1918.
8 Board minutes, February 4, 1918.
9 Board minutes, November 2, 1919.
10 Board minutes, October 23, 1922.
11 Board minutes, June 4, 1923.

Three potential sites were presented to the board in February 1924, and members voted by written ballot. The results were Twenty-Seventh and Mitchell: fifteen votes; Twenty-Eighth and Mitchell: two votes; and Thirtieth and Mitchell: one vote.[12] In March, the congregation voted to purchase the property at Twenty-Seventh and Mitchell for $9,000.[13] A committee was appointed to begin work on plans for the new building. Planning became more detailed in October 1925, when the board appointed two additional committees to guide the building process: a building committee to oversee planning and construction and a finance committee to secure the necessary funding.[14]

Preliminary plans for the new building were approved in May 1926. It was to be seventy-five feet wide and ninety feet long with a full basement and an auditorium (sanctuary) above the basement. There would also be a balcony, classrooms, a choir room, and an organ room.[15] Just over a year-and-a-half later, the board approved final plans for the building,[16] and in March 1928, a construction contract was awarded to Lehr Construction Company.[17]

Making the first payment to the general contractor proved to be a challenge, prompting the board to approve a plan to raise $10,000 "at once." Donations were sought from church members with the goal being one hundred members contributing $100 each (subsequent meeting minutes give no indication as to the success of that campaign).[18] A few weeks later, the board voted to seek a $35,000 loan "at the best terms possible," and it voted to sell "the old church building at the best price possible."[19] Both objectives were accomplished, with modifications. A loan of $30,000 (6 percent interest) was secured from American National Bank, but more was needed, so several board

---

12 Board minutes, February 11, 1924.
13 Board minutes, March 16, 1924.
14 Board minutes, October 5, 1925.
15 Board minutes, May 17, 1926.
16 Board minutes, December 12, 1927.
17 Board minutes, March 19, 1928.
18 Board minutes, May 21, 1928.
19 Board minutes, June 13, 1928.

members agreed to lend the church money: H. N. Stevenson, H. L. Dannen, L. D. Gill, Dr. O. G. Weed, Pete Comello, W. J. Bonsall, W. E. Garlichs, and G. B. Womack.[20] As for the "old church building" at Twenty-Seventh and Olive, it was sold for $1,250.[21]

Large building projects typically include some problems, and such was the case with the building project at Twenty-Seventh and Mitchell. Most serious was a problem with trim stone used in multiple locations throughout the building. It had not been properly waterproofed, and leaks started to appear almost immediately after the trim was installed. The problem was eventually resolved but not before many letters went back and forth between the pastor, building committee, contractor, and architect.[22] Construction progressed and the new church building was dedicated in October 1928.

MOVING TO TWENTY-SEVENTH AND MITCHELL

Dedication of the new building was a protracted affair lasting six days.[23] Three worship services were held Sunday, October 7, 1928, at 10:30 a.m., 2:30 p.m., and 7:30 p.m. Dr. Frederick Kershner of Butler University in Indianapolis spoke at all three services. A Monday evening service was led by Christian Endeavor (youth) groups, and Tuesday evening featured an "Organ Recital and Dedication of the Two Manual Geneva Organ." Worship services were held during each of the remaining evenings, through Friday. Dr. C. M. Chilton, pastor of First Christian Church in downtown St. Joseph, was the speaker at the final worship service.[24]

---

20 Board minutes, August 6, 1928.

21 Board minutes, July 8, 1929.

22 Historical file, 1928 Building.

23 Wyatt Park Christian Church, *Programme of Dedicatory Services*, October 7–14, 1928.

24 A newspaper article published on the occasion of the sanctuary dedication in 1957 noted that it was Dr. Chilton's fourth building dedication service at Wyatt Park. He participated in the rededication of the remodeled church building at Twenty-Seventh and Olive in 1902, dedication services for the new church building at Twenty-Seventh and Mitchell in 1928, dedication of the Education Building in 1951, and the sanctuary dedication on November 24, 1957. *St. Joseph News-Press*, November 21, 1957.

Built at a cost of $55,000, the new church building was described in the *St. Joseph News-Press* as follows:

> The new building, which fronts on Mitchell Avenue, is constructed of tan variegated brick, and is classic style in architecture. Entrance to the first floor is on a level with the street. The first floor comprises a large Sunday School assembly room, class rooms, and a fully equipped kitchen. On the second floor is the sanctuary, the pastor's study, and class rooms. The third floor includes the balcony to the sanctuary and more classrooms. In the building there are nineteen class rooms. Woodwork and pews in the sanctuary are finished in walnut and the walls and ceilings are tinted ivory.[25]

When the building was dedicated in October 1928, no one suspected that one year later, in October 1929, the stock market would crash. While that was not the only cause for what came to be known as the Great Depression, the market crash was a major factor. It marked the beginning of several years of economic hardship. Additionally, weather extremes were frequent in the 1930s. Although the worst of the Dust Bowl was a few hundred miles west of St. Joseph, this area suffered through severe drought that was combined with

---

25 *St. Joseph News-Press*, October 7, 1928.

record heat and cold. Many weather records that were set in the 1930s still stand today. Life was difficult for everyone, and the hard times were also felt by the congregation meeting in its new home at Twenty-Seventh and Mitchell.

Routine expenses posed a continual challenge, and there was a building loan to repay. Minutes of multiple meetings in the early and mid-1930s describe discussions about not being able to make a loan payment at all or being able to make only a partial payment or only an interest payment. Loans were refinanced and/or restructured (see "Statement by the Minister" below). A 1933 request made to the denomination's lending agency, the Board of Church Extension, was unsuccessful.[26]

Just getting by was difficult and required creative responses to problems. One example is an idea discussed by the board at the beginning of 1935: "Moved we install an anti-syphoning device approved by underwriters (UL) to oil burner." The minutes do not indicate whether the motion carried.[27] Heating costs were an annual issue, and in response the board periodically reduced the number of days per week that the building could be heated. Once in a while, a new source of revenue arose, an example being requests by other churches to use Wyatt Park's baptistery. A plan was approved by the board to charge one dollar to provide the water and heat it and fifty cents for the custodian's extra duties. In addition, "the building was not to be especially heated for these services."[28]

Repaying building loans remained challenging, but help came in 1936 in the form of a $12,000 loan from the Board of Church Extension.[29] Board member H. N. Stevenson was formally thanked by the board "for the great amount of work he did in arranging for this loan."[30] Payments were more

---

26 Board minutes, May 1, 1933.

27 Board minutes, January 1935 (exact date is not indicated).

28 Board minutes, September 1939 (exact date is not indicated).

29 Special Congregational Meeting Minutes, January 26, 1936.

30 Board minutes, March 1936 (exact date is not indicated). A story has been handed down through the years that one (or more) church members traveled to the Board of Church Extension (presumably to Indianapolis, since that is where the BCE was, and still is, headquartered). As the story goes, in order to secure the loan, the church members took out second mortgages on their homes. The story is certainly plausible given the impact the Great

manageable under the new financing plan, although they still proved difficult. Wyatt Park was not alone among churches struggling to make loan payments during the Depression. In response, "the Board of Church Extension
forgave over $1 million in principal and interest on its own loans."[31] Wyatt
Park was a beneficiary of that decision, although the exact amount that was
forgiven by the Board of Church Extension is unknown. What *is* known is
that the church's finances eventually improved and payments resumed in
the early 1940s. The Board of Church Extension was repaid, including the
amount that had been forgiven,[32] and a "mortgage burning ceremony" was
held in March 1943.[33] As it turned out, however, the congregation was not yet
finished paying for the building it had dedicated in 1928.

"A Moral Obligation"

Following the Great Depression and World War II, the congregation's
finances improved considerably, so much so that it was faced with a moral
dilemma. Rev. Lawrence Bash offered a solution during a sermon on January
20, 1946. His message was summarized in the worship bulletin the following
week under the heading "A Statement by the Minister," and his statement is
quoted in its entirety:

> Last Sunday morning, the minister presented the matter of a "Moral
> Obligation" to the congregation. In the mid-thirties, it was necessary
> to refinance the indebtedness on the new church building. In the
> course of this, those who invested in our bonds lost about $15,000.
> They accepted about 60 cents on the dollar. There was no alternative

---

Depression had on everyone, but I have not found documentation indicating that any church
members took out second mortgages on their homes in order to secure a loan for the church.

31 Board of Church Extension, *BCExtension* Newsletter, Fall, 1986.

32 Ibid.

33 *St. Joseph News-Press*, n.p. Exact date of the article from 1943 is unknown. Board minutes, February 7, 1943, include plans for the upcoming mortgage burning ceremony "sometime in March."

to this course which was brought about by the financial disaster now known as the Depression. The discounting of our bonds would not have been necessary if the members of the church had not themselves lost large sums of money in the debacle. Investments of every kind suffered severely. The church took the only course open, a practice of many churches and other institutions.

However, the past few years have seen an unheard of prosperity come to the church. Not only have the budgets for local expenses and missions tripled and quadrupled; in addition, we have laid aside more than $17,000 in a building fund. The contrast between the hard necessity of the 30's and this period of prosperity has been too much for the conscience of the church. It was felt that something should be done to make restitution. The repaying of the original investors proved unfeasible for a number of reasons. Therefore, the board has authorized setting up a "conscience fund" into which, it is hoped, we may pour some $15,000 in the coming years. Since the obligation is strictly moral, all legal necessities having been met, it was felt that the money should be used in accord with moral principles. Where should such a sum of money be expended? There are three possibilities before us: (1) it may be used through the World Council of Churches to build a temporary church for some German city without worship facilities; (2) it may be used through the United Christian Missionary Society [one of the terms by which the denomination was known in the 1940s] to rebuild a mission church or property in China; (3) it may be used to assist the Frederick Avenue Church of this city in building a new building. The decision of where the money is to go will be guided by the people of the congregation. In addition, our new Living Link missionary[34] will be sustained from this fund.

This is an attempt by the church to go "beyond the law" and to live by higher standards than the world at large. We do not owe this money in any legal sense. But we will feel better to pay it, and to put it

---

34 The "Living Link Missionary" was Allin Sharp who served in Paraguay. See chapter 6.

into some worthy work. These projects are such as any church should find joy and inspiration in. The fund will be handled through our missionary treasury. Lump sums will be accepted at any time; but it is thought that most people will prefer to increase their missionary giving to the point that at least $2,000 will be made available for this purpose each year for the coming six or seven years. The Christmas offering of over $1,500 will be regarded as a "down payment" on the fund.

In order to approach the problem unselfishly, our own building program is temporarily postponed. For the coming few months, there will be no appeal for the building fund, though gifts may be made to that fund at any time, as you may wish.[35]

It is not possible to determine exactly how money given to the "conscience fund" was used, but financial records in subsequent years indicate considerable generosity toward the needs discussed in Rev. Bash's statement, along with many others. A commitment to missions, to generously sharing the gospel and the blessings of God, is evident in the congregation today, but it is not new. That generous spirit goes back many decades.

"TEACHING THEM TO OBSERVE"

Carved in the stone above the Twenty-Seventh Street entrance are the words "Teaching Them To Observe." That entrance is part of an addition that was dedicated in 1951, but the three-story portion of the building actually consists of two sections constructed more than twenty years apart. The front section (with the sign facing Mitchell Avenue) was dedicated in 1928 and was connected to the old sanctuary. The larger section was added in 1951 at a cost of $140,000, but the process of constructing it began in the fall of 1943.

Growing membership in the early 1940s prompted the trustees to recommend a building fund drive and consultation with an architect about possible

---

35 Worship bulletin, January 27, 1946.

additions to the building.[36] World War II affected almost every area of life, including the congregation's effort to raise funds for building expansion. A folder describing ways members could contribute to the Building Expansion Fund had these words on its cover: "In the Midst of War—We Build for Peace." Members were invited to contribute cash, purchase war bonds in the name of the church, or donate war stamps that could be converted to Series F bonds. A tentative goal of $20,000 was set by the church board.[37] Donations were received for just over two years, until the fund drive was suspended for a time following Rev. Bash's January 1946 statement about the formation of the "conscience fund." Eleven months later, the congregation was again invited to contribute to the building fund, but even though more than a year had passed since the end of World War II, it still had an impact, as noted in the church newsletter: "Building would be impossible just now. Houses are desperately needed by veterans, and costs of labor and material are 'out of sight.' But the day will come, how soon none of us knows, when building will be possible. When that day comes, we must be ready to go."[38]

By March 1949, the board concluded the day had come, and it authorized the Building Planning Committee to make plans for construction.[39] One year later, almost to the day, plans had been approved, bids were accepted, and the board voted to begin construction at once.[40] Construction progressed well, such that the cornerstone was laid in June 1950. Included in the cornerstone were mementos from several classes and groups within the church.[41] Unfortunately, war again affected construction. Fighting in Korea made labor and materials harder to get, slowing construction a bit.[42] Nevertheless, construction continued, and in March 1951, the building addi-

---

36 Board minutes, September 1943 (exact date is not indicated).

37 Building expansion fund folder, *In the Midst of War—We Build for Peace*, filed with worship bulletins, 1943.

38 *The Call to Worship*, November 28, 1946.

39 *The Call to Worship*, March 10, 1949.

40 *The Call to Worship*, March 2, 1950.

41 *Yearbook Directory*, 1950–1951.

42 *The Call to Worship*, September 21, 1950.

tion was dedicated. In a 1951 brochure describing the new addition, Rev. Tom Toler wrote these words:

> This new building shall become an increasingly effective tool of Christian Education. Through its doors, for years to come, bright-eyed, eager boys and girls will come for guidance in the finer things of life. Within its walls, adults will find fellowship and help in Christian living. The things of honesty, truth and justice; of love, hope, and Christian faith will be made to live in the lives of those to whom this building will open its hospitable doors. Thus, through Christian Education at its best, the Wyatt Park Christian Church will minister to the lives of boys and girls, men and women.[43]

When the building addition was dedicated in 1951, there were multiple, grade-level Sunday- School classes for children and older youth and seven classes for adults. Through the years, there have been many changes in the ways particular rooms are used, but the purpose of that part of the facility remains the same today as it was then: "Teaching Them To Observe."

"THE SANCTUARY BEAUTIFUL"

Its shape has been described as being like that of a blimp hangar or an upside-down ark. Most of the time, it is described as *beautiful*. "It" is the sanctuary, a structure that is unique in northwest Missouri and can rightly be called a work or art. Since 1957, Wyatt Park folk have gathered in that exquisite space multiple times each week for worship, and it has been the location for countless weddings, funerals, concerts, musicals, and special services. Dedicated in 1957, the sanctuary's story—at least formally—goes back to 1954.

Three years after the dedication of the building addition in 1951, a Building Improvements Committee was at work studying options for the congregation's worship space. Multiple problems with the existing sanctuary were

---

43 Wyatt Park Christian Church, *The Church for the Whole Family*, March 4–11, 1951.

noted by the committee: (1) the congregation had outgrown it; (2) entering required worshippers to climb many steps, effectively prohibiting the "aged and infirm" from worshiping; and (3) it was not air-conditioned and the addition of cooling equipment would be extremely expensive.[44] In consultation with an architect from the Board of Church Extension, the committee considered three options. Two of those options involved construction of a new sanctuary west of the existing facility. Scheme A featured a new sanctuary, architecturally similar to the existing facility. It would face north with an entrance door into the narthex (area immediately outside the sanctuary) directly off Mitchell Avenue. Scheme C also featured a new sanctuary with "entirely new architectural lines."[45] It would face south, and the main entrance would be near the southwest corner of the Education Building.

A third option was to remodel the existing sanctuary by expanding it to the north wall, eliminating several classrooms. New classroom space would be included in an extension to the west of the Education Building.[46] Anyone worshiping at Wyatt Park today can readily recognize that the committee chose Scheme C. Committee chairman Roger Pope presented the recommendation

to the board at its September meeting, and it was approved unanimously.[47] Construction cost was estimated at $150,000, but that turned out to be $100,000 too low.

An architect was chosen by the board the following spring, and by late October, a model of the proposed sanctuary was on display for church members to view prior to a congregational meeting.[48] A newsletter article noted that the proposed design was contemporary in architecture:

---

44 Building Improvements Committee Minutes, August 24, 1954.
45 For reasons not noted in these minutes, there was no Scheme B.
46 Building Improvements Committee Minutes, August 24, 1954.
47 *The Call to Worship*, September 16, 1954.
48 *The Call to Worship*, April 14, 1955.

That is, it represents the time in which the people live who are erecting the building, rather than a carryover from some past period of history or culture. The shape is parabolic, one of the oldest types of construction, and also one of the strongest. Furthermore, the contemporary design was seen as more cost-efficient.

While the sanctuary design is unique in northwest Missouri, a church building of similar design in Wichita, Kansas provided inspiration for the creation of Wyatt Park's worship space. A bell tower would be constructed at the southeast corner of the sanctuary. As noted in the newsletter, "The top of the tower would be 64 feet, the cross would soar 88 feet above the ground." [49]

On Wednesday evening, November 2, 1955, those attending a congregational meeting gave unanimous approval to the proposed design. In a newsletter article following the vote, some of the building's symbolism was discussed:

For instance: the curved line of the building is suggestive of the up-ward curving lines of "Praying Hands." At the same time, the downward sweep of the arches is representative of the Spirit of God hovering over His people as they gather together to worship. On the interior, the exposed arches are reminiscent of the ribs of a boat and symbolize the earliest conception of the Church which is that it is the Ship of Faith in which God's people sail toward eternity.[50]

Exactly thirteen months after the vote to approve the design, ground was broken for the new sanctuary on December 2, 1956. A newsletter article the following week reported that:

Earth was turned by Mr. Roger Pope, chairman of the Building Planning Committee; Mr. Ralph Sawyer, chairman of the Church Board, in behalf of the congregation; Mrs. W.J. Clark, president of

---

49 *The Call to Worship*, October 26, 1955.
50 *The Call to Worship*, September 11, 1955.

the CWF, in behalf of the women of the church; Mr. Earl Johnson, Church School Superintendent, and by the minster [Tom Toler].[51]

Once ground was broken, construction got underway quickly. It progressed steadily over the next eleven months, although there is surprisingly little detail about the construction in the newsletters during that time, and no photos. Of course, church members saw the progress each time they came on the property so they would have been well aware of progress, or lack thereof. Although construction progressed well, there were some hitches along the way. For example, one of the laminated arches fell as it was being set in place. It was damaged beyond repair, so another arch had to be shipped from Seattle.[52] Because of the sanctuary's unique design, the construction project drew plenty of onlookers and attention from the *St. Joseph News-Press*, which printed multiple stories about the sanctuary's construction. By the end of the first week of June, the sanctuary was "closed in," with the roofing all in place. On Sunday, June 2, 1957, a special ceremony was held to place the marble cornerstone.

Construction continued through the summer and fall, and the sanctuary was dedicated on Sunday, November 24, 1957. That was the first day the sanctuary was used, and what a day it was. More than one thousand people attended the two morning services, and hundreds attended the dedication service at 3:00 p.m. The dedication service opened with the hymn "God of Grace and God of Glory" and closed with "Lead On, O King Eternal." In between was music, scripture, greetings from sister churches, prayers, and a litany of dedication.[53] The minister, Dr. Tom Toler, shared a message not only celebrating the occasion but also reminding the congregation of the purpose:

We have not built here, I hope, a monument to our pride or prosperity. We have simply sought to express our love, our faith, our hope in God through brick, wood, and glass. All around us, then today, is the language of our worship. This building has been built with only one

---

51 *The Call to Worship*, December 5, 1956.

52 *The Call to Worship*, May 8, 1957.

53 Dedication program, November 24, 1957. The Call to Worship, December 1, 1957.

purpose in mind; that those who come here might be helped to worship God—and through their worship find their lives lifted, changed, and filled with power.[54]

Initially estimated to cost $150,000, the sanctuary was constructed at a cost of $255,000, including $15,000 for the *Creation Window* and $17,000 for the organ.[55]

Construction of the organ was plagued by multiple problems. James Lawbaugh of St. Joseph was contracted to design and build the organ, and "the organ which was used in the older sanctuary was used as the basic instrument upon which to build the new one."[56] The organ was dedicated during a worship service in January 1959, despite the fact that it was incomplete. Multiple letters between the trustees, the contractor, and attorneys reveal a very tense relationship. Exactly when and how the relationship ended is unclear, but it was announced in October 1960 that Midwest Organ Service would complete construction of "The Pipe Organ, 'orphaned' in the midst of construction."[57] The organ was finally completed on March 1, 1963, and debuted to an overflow crowd on March 3, 1963, for a recital sponsored by the Organist Guild. An information page prepared for that occasion described the organ:

The organ console, manufactured in 1957 by the M.P. Moller Co. of Hagarstown, Maryland is located against the south wall of the chancel area. The console houses a separate keyboard or manual for each of the four divisions of the organ. In addition to the 215 keys, there are 42 Stop Knobs which select the various sounds to be heard. 23 Couplers with which the organist may combine the various divisions of the organ, and 39 Pistons which can be pre-set at the organist's

---

54 Dr. Tom Toler, *Brick, Wood, and Glass—The Language of Worship*, a sermon preached on the occasion of the dedication of the new sanctuary, November 24, 1957. "New Building" files.

55 "Contracts" file within "New Building" files.

56 *The Call to Worship*, January 14, 1959.

57 *The Call to Worship*, January 20, 1960.

will to select instantaneously any given combination of Stops and Couplers…a total of 319 console controls.

Each division of the organ is in reality a distinct organ in itself. The pipes of the "Choir Organ," controlled by the bottom manual at the console, are located in an expression chamber high in the east wall of chancel at the front of the sanctuary.

The "Great Organ," controlled by the second manual, is exposed in the rear gallery. The sound of exposed pipes can support congregational singing more effectively.

The "Swell Organ," controlled by the top manual, is located in the expression chamber to the east of the gallery organ at the rear of the sanctuary.

The pipework of the "Pedal Organ," controlled by the foot pedal keys at the console, is distributed between the chambers of the other divisions of the organ. The tallest pipes, which may be seen at the rear in the Great Organ gallery, are in the pedal division. The tallest pipe is over 16 feet long and is made of zinc. Other pipes in the organ are made from brass, wood, and various alloys of tin, lead, and zinc.

Wind for the organs is supplied by two blowers located in the basement of the sanctuary, one in the rear and the second in the front [the rear blower was replaced in 2016].

The pipe organ may be likened to a symphony orchestra in that the various pipes produce a wide variety of sounds. The voices of the organ may be divided into the following categories: "Principals," so called as the pipes produce the "principal" or most characteristic sound of a pipe organ; the "Strings," the "Flutes," and the "Reeds," in which brass reeds are blown by the wind. There is a total of 1608 pipes in this instrument.[58]

Other problems persisted. In early 1959, the Building Committee prepared a lengthy memo describing unresolved issues. Multiple problems were found in

---

58 "The Organ," informational page prepared for the occasion of the organ's debut on March 3, 1963.

the heating and air-conditioning system. Roof leaks were evident, the foyer and narthex needed new flooring because of damaged tiles, and there were ongoing problems pertaining to nonpayment of subcontractors by the general contractor.[59] In the years since then, most expenses have been routine in nature, but there have been a few unusual expenditures.

In October 1968, lighting struck the wooden cross on the bell tower. It splintered, and many pieces landed on Mitchell Avenue. A metal cross was installed in July 1969.[60] A storm window was installed in 1972 to protect the *Creation Window*,[61] but it was no match for a car that struck the window in November 2015. Shrubs at the base of the window absorbed much of the force, but two bottom sections of the storm window were broken. The *Creation Window* itself was not damaged.

Exactly fifty years *to the hour* after the sanctuary was first dedicated, it was rededicated at 3:00 p.m., on Saturday, November 24, 2007. Former pastor Dr. Gene Mockabee returned to speak during the service, and the music was a mix of contemporary praise songs and hymns, including two hymns that were sung fifty years earlier at the initial service of dedication. As the sanctuary approaches its sixtieth anniversary, it continues to be used three times each weekend for worship and dozens of times each year for weddings, funerals, and special services. And it is still the same as it was described in a pamphlet published for the dedication service in 1957: "The Sanctuary Beautiful."[62]

THE *CREATION WINDOW*

If there is any part of the church facility that might be considered iconic, it is the *Creation Window*, a work of art to the glory of God. This forty-foot wall of color and light was designed and built by the Emil Frei Stained Glass Studio in St. Louis. Robert Frei was the artist, and the window has been featured

---

59 Memo from Building Committee, "Items Pending for Completion of Building as of January 19, 1959." "Committee folder" contained within "New Building" files.

60 *The Call to Worship*, July 24, 1969.

61 Board minutes, August 14, 1972.

62 Pamphlet prepared to accompany the dedication of the sanctuary, November 24, 1957.

in numerous magazine articles and books. Emil Frei and Associates is still in business and continues to use the *Creation Window* in some of its promotional material. Its current President, Stephen Frei (fourth generation to lead the studio), wrote the following about how the *Creation Window* was made:[63]

Your sanctuary window involved considerable painting on "mouth blown, full antique" leaded stained glass crystal. "Full antique" does not describe its age, but rather the method used in blowing it. Full Antique glass has been, and to this day still is, the nicest glass made in the world.

The first step of actually blowing the glass is not done at ours or any other design studio. We buy the base glass in large sheets from mouth blowing companies all over the world.

Almost all stained glass was blown free form in the air from the twelfth through nineteenth centuries. A solid ball of molten glass would be swirled onto the end of a long hollow pipe. Men would then blow into the pipe, starting a giant bubble. Nothing would touch the glass as it was being blown into cylinders prior to flattening. As the glass bubble expanded, stretched, and cooled, all the accidental magical crystalline lines would appear, much like frost starting on the surface of a lake or on a window pane. Once the cylinder reached a size approximately 3 ½ feet long by one foot in diameter, scissors would be used to cut off the still hot base, along with cutting off the other end where it is attached to the blowing pipe. The cylinder would be quickly cooled so it could be cracked down the side, the crack then spread with toothpicks. Afterwards, it would be put back into a kiln and heated to the point the glass cylinder lost its strength, until it would slowly unfold into a sheet of approximately 24 by 36 inches. Once the cooled glass flattened onto the tray, it would essentially be the first time anything of significance, other than air, had touched the surface.

---

63 Stephen Frei's quotes are contained in a letter to the author dated October 24, 2014. Emil Frei Associates, Inc., 1017 West Adams, St. Louis, MO, 63122. Used with permission.

Only a handful of countries in the world mouth blow stained glass and the textures vary from country to country. We use these varieties of textures to help create three dimensional glass sculptures. Our intent for viewers is threefold: when they look at a window they initially see color, then secondly they see subject matter. Finally, once they have become familiar with their windows, they start to notice all the wonderful differences between the glasses (bubbles, crystalline ridges, painting techniques, etc.), so that every time they look, they are constantly discovering new aspects and characters. Combine this with shifting light at various times of the day and a recipe is born for an ever-changing and evolving work of art.

One type of German glass in your window is characterized by many, many little bubbles. These bubbles are put in by throwing a potato into the vat of molten glass prior to blowing. The potato dissolves and explodes with the residue going up the flue. However, this controlled reaction releases bubbles into the glass which are trapped in the taffy-like hot material. Then when the solid ball of molten glass is swirled onto the end of the pipe and blown, the trapped air bubbles are stretched, much like writing on the surface of an expanding balloon.

A glass called Reamy is made in both Germany and France, and is characterized by stronger lines. A glass called Kronos (made in Poland) has almost no textures at all, allowing your vision to pass through the pieces unimpeded.

There are two steps where color is added. Prior to blowing, small amounts of metals are mixed into the molten glass to give the base glass its vibrant colors: cobalt making blues, selaniums making orange and yellows, gold making deep reds, etc. To differentiate, the color of the small individual pieces is determined by cutting them out of the large, colored blown sheets. Painting is then done after the individual pieces are cut.

The majority of the painting in your window was done in blacks, which consists of iron oxide suspended in Acacia gum and water. We do not paint with paint at all, but rather with metal oxides. These metal oxides, which are suspended in the Acacia gum and water (or oil, depending on the textures desired), are applied to the surface. Once applied, the oxides are then kiln fired into the glass at 1,200 degrees Fahrenheit (the melting point of glass) so that the oxides become fused with absolute permanence, never to fade or peel with time.

The glazing processes of leading, sealing, and strengthening the stained glass have changed very little in the last 500 years. We use lead both for its remarkable resistance to corrosion, and for the fact that it is soft. It forms a soft perimeter cushion protecting the edges of each piece from adjacent pieces. This stops any possibility of chips or flakes starting runs or cracks. It is not known how long your stained glass window can be expected to last (as windows elsewhere in the world are now reaching 950 years old and the first created by our studio are now over 100 years old), but barring unusual circumstances (such as fires or tornadoes), our stained glass windows should long outlast any building.

Near the conclusion of his letter, Stephen Frei added some personal thoughts about the uniqueness of the *Creation Window*:

Wyatt Park's monumental window is a cutting-edge standout in the continuing, slow evolution of stained glass. The opportunity given to studios by progressive congregations to step outside of societal norms to create does not come along near often enough. When they do, too often people are engaged that do not have the necessary capabilities or understandings and the commission falls flat. Yours truly is in the forefront of almost all other contemporary churches in the country.

Stephen Frei's letter was written in response to a request for an estimate of what it might cost to replace the window, should the need ever arise. Given the special methods that were used to create it, along with its size and design complexity, the estimated replacement cost as of October 2014 was $392,415.

While the beauty of the *Creation Window* can be appreciated without knowing the meaning behind what is depicted within it, the window is loaded with symbolism. What follows is from the pamphlet (noted above) that was prepared for the sanctuary's dedication in 1957:

The Creation Window speaks of the continual creative power of God in human life and the universe. With this in mind, the viewer looks upward to find a stream of colorful light flowing down from the top-most point of the arch and toward the east. This shaft of light and color, representing the creative spirit of God, first passes through a symbol of the sun, moon, and stars; for the first creative gift of God was light. Flowing down from the source of light is a cone of color; God's gift of beauty through light.

As the eye moves downward a flame of fire is seen; another of God's great gifts. Fire has both physical and spiritual importance, for it was through the flaming bush that God spoke to Moses. Fire is also a symbol of God's continuing presence through the Holy Spirit.

The creating of humankind is depicted in a triangle of pale blue color as a reminder that our lives consist of three things: body, mind, and spirit. In the triangle are set jeweled likenesses of tools which people have devised through the ages. An evergreen tree can be seen near the center of the window; a symbol of God's gift of vegetation that sustains the physical life. There is a spiritual meaning as well, and that is the hope for everlasting life.

Near the tree a boat may be seen with waves of water in the background. Water is one of the essential gifts of God to humankind. The boat also reminds us of the Noah story and the salvation of his kindred in the ark. For Christians, the Church is our ship of faith in which we sail through the seas of life. Near the base of the window, stalks of wheat may be seen which tell of God's gift of His Son, Jesus, "the bread of life."

All of these gifts have been given by our loving, gracious, creative God. What are we to do with them? Are we to keep them to ourselves? No! We are to take all that God has given to us and offer it back to Him in prayer, praise, worship, love, and service. Therefore, a great shaft of light flows back upward as we offer up our spirits and our lives to God.

And then we may notice something we did not see before. At the top of the window, at the point where our spirits encounter the Spirit of God, there is a cross, and thus it must ever be. We meet God at the Cross of Christ.[64]

---

64 Pamphlet prepared to accompany the dedication of the sanctuary, November 24, 1957 (paraphrased). The Creation Window was the inspiration for a choral anthem that debuted at Wyatt Park in February 2005. "The Colors of Your Grace" was written by Kansas City

TEMPORARY = TWENTY-SIX YEARS

Wyatt Park Christian Church has a long history of responding to changing circumstances, so it is no surprise that the facility has been changed multiple times through the years. Ten years after dedicating the sanctuary, the congregation voted in 1967 to approve another plan for renovation and expansion, a plan that was two years in the making.

Multiple issues had been identified, including the need for renovation of the three-story Education Building and the addition of classroom and meeting space. There was also the question of what to do with the old sanctuary. A Building Plans Committee chaired by Charles Salanski developed a multipoint plan that was intended to be long-range and completed in stages. Board approval came in November 1966, and the architect was instructed to prepare final plans for stage one.[65] Included in the initial stage were renovation of the Education Building and the addition of new space behind it along Twenty-Seventh Street. That new space today includes the Fireside Room, a classroom, and kitchenette as well as the youth area on the lower level. Intended as a *temporary* Social Hall, the lower level space was used that way for nearly twenty-six years. New and enlarged parking areas were included, along with an expanded rear (west) entrance to the sanctuary (essentially where the Children's Media Center is today). Removal of the old sanctuary was included, and designers envisioned a "corner chapel" being built in its place. Sadly, while the old sanctuary was razed, the small circular chapel was never constructed. It would have been located in what today is the grass area that includes the lighted sign.[66]

Lawhon Construction Company completed the project at a cost of $287,000, and a special dedication service was held on Sunday, May 26, 1968.[67]

---

composer Mark Hayes and was commissioned by a church member to honor the music ministry of Darren Verbick.

65 *The Call to Worship*, November 17, 1966.
66 *The Call to Worship*, August 3, 1967.
67 *The Call to Worship*, May 9, 1968 and May 16, 1968.

Neither Rain Nor Snow

People entering the church from the parking lots on the west side immediately see the Social Hall on the left and the offices straight ahead. That is the newest part of the facility, built at a cost of $1,200,000 and dedicated in 1994. Although plans for the Social Hall dated back to 1968, it was another twenty-five years before construction actually began. In addition to the Social Hall and offices, the 1993–1994 construction project also included the Atrium, the large yellow room downstairs, and the canopy over the "circle drive" entrance on Mitchell Avenue.

A "General Consultation" report from the denomination's Board of Church Extension was shared with leaders of the congregation in September 1989. That report focused on facility needs and methods of financing construction.[68] A "Study and Plans Committee" report in 1990 added more details, and in 1992 a fund-raising effort was undertaken.[69] A combination of donations and a mortgage loan financed the project that got underway in 1993.

Construction took longer than originally anticipated because of heavy rains and flooding in 1993. Dr. Gene Mockabee, Senior Pastor, wrote a newsletter column acknowledging the impact of flooding on the region and on construction at Wyatt Park: "We have been hoping to have a big Thanksgiving Dinner in the new Social Hall before Thanksgiving. Someone has reminded me recently that *whenever* we get into the new Social Hall we can have a *Thanksgiving* Dinner."[70] That dinner finally took place eleven months later.

By the summer of 1994, the project was completed, and on June 19, 1994, the new facilities were dedicated. Former pastors Tom Toler and Lawrence Bash were in attendance, and Rev. Kyle Maxwell, a "Timothy" of the church, was the featured speaker.[71] The mortgage loan was finally paid off in January 2013.

---

68 Administrative Cabinet minutes, September 18, 1989.

69 Study and Plans Committee report, January 1990.

70 *The Call to Worship*, July 8, 1993.

71 The term "Timothy" is used to refer to someone who grew up in a congregation and then went forth from that congregation to work in some field of ministry.

A Few More...

Some details of the facility are noteworthy but are not connected with one of the phases of construction. Here are some examples:

Prayer Rooms:

There have been at least two prayer rooms, the earliest of which was described briefly in a 1958 newsletter article. It was on the third floor of the Education Building and was developed by the Christian Youth Fellowship (CYF-high school) and Chi-Rho (junior high) youth groups. It featured a worship center "finished in oak with a walnut cross on the front."[72]

Forty-one years later, in 1999, a new Prayer Chapel was created in a room just off the Friendship Area. Charlene Russell, Ali Wray, and Cindy Clinch led the effort to create the space for prayer and meditation. Several artisans were also involved, creating a kneeling bench, a wooden cross, and stained glass windows for the doors.[73]

In 2008, Wyatt Park hosted some visitors from Mexico who were here as guests of the Northwest Area of the Christian Church in Mid-America (denominational region). They were especially taken with the Prayer Chapel, which they referred to as the "Power Center." Indeed it is, or as the apostle Paul put it in his letter to the Philippians, "Do not be anxious about anything, but in everything by prayer and supplication with thanksgiving let your requests be made known to God. And the peace of God, which surpasses all understanding, will guard your hearts and your minds in Christ Jesus" (Phil. 4:6–7).

Last Supper Painting:

Paintings of the Last Supper that Jesus shared with his disciples are found in many church buildings. Most are prints of Leonardo da Vinci's late fifteenth-century mural at a convent in Milan, Italy. Also popular, although less so, is Salvador Dali's 1955 painting of the Last Supper. In the circle drive entry area facing Mitchell Avenue hangs an original painting of the Last Supper, a unique work of art that has graced the walls of Wyatt Park Christian Church since 1935.

---

72 *The Call to Worship*, May 7, 1958.

73 Board minutes, October 18, 1999.

It was painted by Eugene McFarland, a member of Wyatt Park from 1933 until 1938, when he left St. Joseph for a teaching position at Phillips University in Enid, Oklahoma. McFarland was a devoted Christian who was born in St. Louis in 1908. A teacher and painter, he was primarily known for his paintings of the American frontier. His unique depiction of the Last Supper originally hung behind the communion table in the old sanctuary. He gave the painting to the church in memory of his father, who was a minister in the Christian Church for many years. After the new sanctuary was dedicated, the painting was moved to the church library and then to the narthex where it hung for many years. When the narthex was remodeled in 2016, the painting was moved to its current location, in the circle drive entry area.

Eugene McFarland died in an auto accident in 1955 near Wichita, Kansas, where he had served as director of the Wichita Art Museum.[74]

God's Garden:
Between the two parking lots on the west side of the building is a small garden. Tended by different groups of volunteers through the years, it has been known in recent years as God's Garden. It was given that name in 2006 by Charlene Russell and the half-dozen youth who worked with her to care for it.[75]

Its *roots* go back to the mid-twentieth century when an old garage was torn down. Long-time 50-50 Sunday-School class members Walter and Orpha Wilson took the lead in establishing and caring for the garden.[76] Decades after the garden was established, it continues to be an oasis of natural beauty between the west side parking lots.

Parsonages:
During the early and middle decades of the twentieth century, the church provided housing for the Senior Minister. Usually referred to as "parsonages,"

---

74 *The Call to Worship*, March 12, 1970. Also consulted, http://www.askart.com/artist_bio/Eugene_James_McFarland/110479/Eugene_James_McFarland.aspx.
75 *The Call to Worship*, May 10, 2006.
76 *The Call to Worship*, October 2, 2007.

the houses were in the neighborhood around the church. Provision of a parsonage ended in December 1967, when the last of the parsonages was sold.[77]

Pianos:
Finally, there is this item from board minutes in March 1964, a recommendation from the Property Committee: "Mr. [Ross] Woodbury also moved that we enter into a yearly contract with Mr. Bill Sales to tune fifteen pianos in the church building twice a year, with tuning of the grand piano on special occasions, at an annual cost of $75.00. This met with Board approval."[78] Fifteen pianos? That's what it says.

ONE BUILDING, FIVE PARTS
When looking at the church facility today, what is seen is a building that includes five sections, built over a span of nearly seventy years:

1928—front section of the three-story Education Building. It includes the "Wyatt Park Christian Church" sign that faces Mitchell Avenue and was connected to the old sanctuary.
1951—the three-story Education Building addition.
1957—the sanctuary.
1968—Fireside Room, classroom, "kitchenette," and lower level room used today as the high-school youth room.
1994—Social Hall, offices, Atrium, basement multipurpose room, front canopy entrance.

Inside this facility, faithful people of all ages gather for worship, education, and fellowship. It is a place where spiritual nourishment and growth may be found and from which children, youth, and adults go out into the world to live and serve in Jesus's name.

---

77 Real estate contract, 2302 Strader Ter., December 9, 1967, in "Parsonage" folder.
78 Board minutes, March 1964 (exact date is not indicated).

CHAPTER 3

Gathered for Worship

———

God is spirit, and those who worship him must
worship in spirit and truth. (John 4:24)

WYATT PARK FOLK REGULARLY GATHER "beyond the window" for a variety of
reasons, but the primary reason is worship. During worship, the focus is on
God. In terms of importance, no other activity comes close. Education, fellowship, and service are all important, but they must be grounded in a spirit of
worship if they are to be done in ways that truly honor God and bear fruit for
Christ. Because worship "in spirit and truth" is God-centered, it enables us to
encounter God in ways that cannot be experienced in any other setting. That
is not to say encounters with God are *impossible* apart from corporate worship.
They are possible. Rather, it is to say that our encounters with God take on
special significance during worship because they occur as we are gathered
together with people just like us—human beings given life by God, stained
by sin, and in need of a restored relationship with our Creator. When believers gather together in Christ's name, the Lord Himself promises to be present:
"For where two or three are gathered in my name, there I am among them"
(Matt. 18:20).

Throughout its history, the congregation of Wyatt Park Christian Church
has gathered for worship at least once a week. Styles and methods have
changed, but the basic elements of worship have remained the same. Each worship service includes prayers, readings from scripture, congregational singing

and/or special music, the Lord's Supper, and a sermon. Regarding the Lord's Supper (also known as "communion"), weekly observance of the Supper is a hallmark of Wyatt Park's roots in the Campbell-Stone reform movement. Alexander Campbell advocated for weekly observance of the Lord's Supper because he understood that to be the practice of first-century Christians. He specifically cited Acts 20:7, which speaks of "the first day of the week, when we were gathered together to break bread." Campbell took that as a reference to the Lord's Supper and advocated observance of the Supper as an element of weekly worship.

Changes in cultural tastes and styles, along with advances in technology, have influenced the *feel* of worship. What is now referred to as *traditional* worship was considered *normal* worship for the first one hundred plus years of Wyatt Park's existence and is still preferred by some worshippers today. Within that style of worship is music rooted in the classics from centuries past. These days, most of the people who worship at Wyatt Park attend services with music that has a more contemporary feel, is led by the Praise Team, and includes words projected on a screen rather than read from a hymnal.

Expectations about attire have also changed. Until the latter part of the twentieth century, people were expected to "dress up" for worship, meaning suits and ties for men and dresses for women. Appropriate attire is still preferred, but the definition of "appropriate" has relaxed a good bit during the last quarter-century.

Worship language has become less formal as well. Until 1952, the language of worship was heavily influenced by the King James Version of the Bible, published in 1611. Its influence is illustrated by this message of greetings on the front of a Wyatt Park Christian Church worship bulletin from 1928:

> This church offers a hearty welcome to every stranger who may cross its portals. It invites every earnest soul to accept the privilege of prayer and praise and the spiritual good ever to be found in its worship. It invites to its membership all who believe that Jesus Christ is the Divine Son of God and who for themselves purpose lives of service

according to the pattern of His life and teachings. Come and be one of us in this spiritual communion, whose value to us is worship, and whose demonstration to the world is a life of good works. And whosoever thou art who worship in this church, enter it not without the spirit of reverence, and leave it not without one prayer to God for thyself, for him who ministers, and those who worship here.[1]

Worship language changed noticeably with the publication of the Revised Standard Version (RSV) of the Bible in 1952. Its publication was described in *The Call to Worship* as "the most important event in Biblical history in the past 341 years. Here is the Bible, written in the living language we use today—a Bible everyone can read, understand, and enjoy."[2] Since the RSVs publication in 1952, many other English language translations have been published. In 1989, the Revised Standard Version was replaced by the New Revised Standard Version (NRSV).

The "greetings" found on the bulletin noted above speak to the necessity of a "spirit of reverence." "Reverence" has to do with deep respect for something or someone, and it is a key word in understanding preferences for what are considered appropriate styles in worship music, dress, and so forth. Style of dress and music are outward expressions of reverence, but one may dress well or sing classical music without being *inwardly* reverent. Reverence is a matter of the heart.

Rev. Lawrence Bash spoke of this truth when he wrote an article in the *Call to Worship* in 1947. His pulpit attire was the subject:

Next Sunday our minister expects to blossom out in "tails." This is a move that has long been contemplated. There are many opinions on the subject of the pulpit dress. In most larger churches, a cutaway or robes are worn. It is doubtful if they ever improve the sermon. Their

---

1 Worship bulletin, March 4, 1928.

2 *The Call to Worship*, September 18, 1952. Copies of the RSV were placed in the pews in 1953, and they remained until 2008 when they were replaced by the TNIV Bibles that are currently in use.

use simply lends a certain dignity to the pulpit. Your minister has always made a practice of wearing black or navy blue in the pulpit. There is no scriptural precedent for this; it is just a matter of what seems to him "good taste." The cutaway should be classified in the same way. It certainly will do nothing for the sermon. But it is a mark of respect for the pulpit of the church and we hope it will be received in that spirit.[3]

If photos of Wyatt Park pastors accurately reflect what was worn while preaching, then the attire was suits and ties until the mid-twentieth century when robes became common. By the beginning of the twenty-first century, the pastor's attire had transitioned to a suit or sport coat for *traditional* worship and a button-down shirt and slacks for *contemporary praise* worship. Of course, to quote Lawrence Bash, what the pastor wears "certainly will do nothing for the sermon." An effective sermon is grounded in a spirit of reverence for God, for the gospel of Jesus Christ, and for the privilege of teaching in the church. Reverence is a matter of the heart.

Hymns and Anthems

Music sets the tone for worship, and throughout much of Wyatt Park's history, the tone of worship was formal and classical—"traditional," in other words. While one of the three weekend services that are currently offered may be considered traditional, it is less formal and classical than in years past. Special music (e.g., solos) has often been a feature of worship at Wyatt Park, but for the most part, traditional worship music has been in the form of congregational hymns and anthems sung by a choir.

---

3 *The Call to Worship*, February 13, 1947. For many years, *The Call to Worship* published the topic of each upcoming weekend's sermon. Most of those entries are routine, but this notice from November 1946 is an interesting and humorous exception: "The minister does not yet know what his topic will be Sunday, but he will try to have something worthy of saying." *The Call to Worship*, November 14, 1946.

Little is known about what, if any, hymnals were used by the congregation early on, but hymn books were common by the late nineteenth century, so it is likely that some type of song book was used. A worship bulletin from March 1928 (cited above) includes page numbers with the listing of hymns. Several old hymnals are found in bookshelves around the facility today, but when, or even if, they were used during worship is impossible to determine.

As noted above, there was excitement when the Revised Standard Version of the Bible was released in 1952. Not surprisingly, there was also excitement the next year when a new hymnal was published using texts from the RSV. *Christian Worship* was published by the Bethany Press, the Disciples of Christ publishing house. It contained hymns and a variety of worship resources such as prayers, responsive readings, and so forth. With its maroon cover, *Christian Worship* quickly became a familiar sight in Disciples of Christ congregations, including Wyatt Park where the new hymnals were dedicated in October 1953.[4] *Christian Worship* remained the hymnal of choice for Disciples of Christ congregations until 1995 when *The Chalice Hymnal* was published. It included many new songs, along with revised wording of older hymns. Copies of *The Chalice Hymnal* were placed in the pews at Wyatt Park in 1996. Hymnal use declined by the late 1990s with the advent of contemporary praise worship that featured new music and words on a screen.

Concerns about the revised wording of hymns as well as the absence of some favorite songs of worship prompted a decision to remove *The Chalice Hymnal* from the pews in 2015. In its place are copies of *The Celebration Hymnal*, a nondenominational hymnal that includes more of the familiar hymns as well as familiar wording.

Congregational singing is a major element of worship regardless of style, but until as recently as 2013, "traditional" worship at Wyatt Park also featured anthems sung by a choir. Few details are known about Wyatt Park's choirs in the earliest years, but they were a part of worship, and at least some of the members were paid. Consider this from board minutes in 1919: "Brother Hillix reports that [the] choir needs a man to sing tenor and suggested that

---

4 *The Call to Worship*, October 22, 1953.

one be hired. He stated further that [the] choir would undertake to pay his salary. Moved and seconded that the music committee procure a man and that the choir be informed that the Board would guarantee [the] expense for 4 months. Carried."[5] There is no indication of the amount he would be paid.

Few photos exist from those earliest days, but this photo of the "Surpliced Choir" is dated April 3, 1926. The word "surplice" refers to the white vestments worn by choir members. Photos of early choirs show adults. How, or whether, children and youth were involved in early worship at Wyatt Park is unknown. That may have started to change in 1942 with the announced formation of a youth choir for ninth to twelfth graders.[6] Interestingly, there is no further mention of

a youth choir until 1946, when this appeared in the newsletter: "Our new Youth Choir will be introduced for the first time next Sunday in the 8:15 service. Directed by Central High's music director, Mr. Marvin Gench, Jr., it has enrolled fifty young people and expects to grow."[7] According to an article the following week, the debut was a success.

Four months later, a Junior Choir was formed for fourth to seventh graders.[8] That choir outgrew the seating capacity of the choir loft, so in 1950, a second junior choir was formed, to be known as The Carolers.[9] By 1953, there were three choirs for children and youth: Carolers, choir for the children; Clef, Choir for Chi Rho (junior high) youth; and the Youth Choir, for high-school students. Participation in the Carolers and Clef choirs was so large that membership was closed "as it is impossible to robe and seat more members for

---

5 Board minutes, May 5, 1919.
6 Worship bulletin, February 15, 1942.
7 *The Call to Worship*, October 10, 1946.
8 *The Call to Worship*, February 27, 1947.
9 *The Call to Worship*, January 26, 1950.

these choirs."[10] Those two choirs continued into the 1970s and were even featured on KFEQ-TV (channel 2) on Good Friday in 1967 and again in 1968.[11] Changing tastes and lifestyles in the final third of the twentieth century impacted all areas of life, including music in the church. Participation in the children's choirs started to decline, and by the mid-1980s, they were no longer meeting on a regular basis. Since then, attempts to bring back a children's choir have been short-lived.

Taste and lifestyle changes impacted the adult choir as well, but it took longer. Adult choir participation ebbed and flowed over the past fifty years, but the long-term trend was downward. A choir sharing anthems has not been a part of weekly traditional worship since 2013, but while there is no longer a choir, vocal music is alive and well. It is different now, and the shift toward today's preferred music style began in a significant way at Wyatt Park in 1970.

"It's the Lord's Thing"

It was in the fall of 1970 when a new singing group was born at Wyatt Park. Taking the name New Generation (New-G for short), the group was made up of high-school and college-age youth. It was directed by Byron

---

10 *The Call to Worship*, September 24, 1953.
11 *The Call to Worship*, March 23, 1967, and April 4, 1968.

Myers, who joined the church music staff in September 1959. Initially described in *The Call to Worship* as a "folk singing group," New G's first presentation was December 13, 1970, during both Sunday worship services.[12] Their well-received presentation was entitled "It's the Lord's Thing." In the years that followed, the group prepared musical presentations that were shared at Wyatt Park, at other churches in this area, and across the country during what would become annual "New-G Tours" each summer. The 1975 tour was typical with church presentations scheduled for Atwood, Kansas; Colorado Springs and Littleton, Colorado; Salt Lake City and Ogden, Utah; Las Vegas, Los Angeles, Bakersfield, and Newport Beach, California; Pampa, Texas; and Oklahoma City, Oklahoma.[13] Not surprisingly, the group grew from an initial membership of 35 to over 130 within ten years. Unfortunately, membership was not all that grew during those years. Tension grew as well.

It has been said that those things that give us our greatest joy can also give us our deepest pain. Most parents would agree with that statement, and many local churches can also attest to its validity. Wyatt Park is one of those churches.

Issues developed between the leadership of the New Generation Singers and the church. Numerous meetings were held, but the issues remained unresolved. In a letter dated February 11, 1980, New-G informed the board and the congregation that the group would leave Wyatt Park. One month later, the pastor of Ashland United Methodist Church announced to his congregation that New-G would begin rehearsing there.[14] In addition to group members, many families associated with the group left Wyatt Park. New-G's departure turned out to be one of the most painful events in Wyatt Park's history, and it left deep wounds that took years to heal, but in time—*and with God's help*—even deep wounds can heal.

Today, New-G continues to rehearse at Ashland United Methodist Church and go on tours each summer. Almost every year since 1980, the group has included youth from Wyatt Park, and, at different times since 1980,

---

12 *The Call to Worship*, December 10, 1970.

13 *The Call to Worship*, July 24, 1975.

14 *The Messenger*, newsletter of Ashland United Methodist Church, March 20, 1980.

adults from the congregation have served as sponsors. Finally, almost every year the group has one of its summer "sing-outs" at Wyatt Park.

COLOR OUTSIDE THE LINES

Merriam-Webster defines something as "contemporary" when it is "marked by characteristics of the present period."[15] By the early 1990s, "contemporary" was used to describe a new style of worship that rapidly gained in popularity. While the term pointed to more than just music, a new style of music set the tone for contemporary worship. Instead of classical hymns featuring an organ and choir, music in a contemporary service is led by a band with guitars, drums, keyboards, and horns. A small group of vocalists leads congregational singing and the words are on a screen, not in a hymnal. Dress is casual for everyone, including the pastor. Sermons intentionally link scripture with daily life. Little, if anything, is said about the institutional church.

Contemporary worship came to Wyatt Park on February 2, 1997, but the seeds for it were sown years earlier. By 1997, two generations of people had grown up listening to rock 'n' roll, so musical tastes were changing throughout the culture, and that change would not be stopped at the church door. At Wyatt Park, the New Generation Singers did much to develop interest in nontraditional worship music, and in fact, some of the people instrumental in beginning contemporary worship in 1996 were alumni of New-G. Interest in a new way to worship became intentional in 1994 when Wyatt Park hosted a conference that featured a pastor from Kentucky.

First Christian Church in Shelbyville, Kentucky, had successfully introduced contemporary worship, and its pastor, Dr. Howard Griffith, came to Wyatt Park in early November to lead a workshop. Forty people attended.[16] By early 1995, a Celebration Team was meeting regularly to consider both a new style of worship and how existing worship services could be improved. Team members attended conferences at churches such as Willow Creek Community

---

15 *Merrian-Webster OnLine,* s.v. "contemporary,"accessed December 19, 2016, https://www.merriam-webster.com/dictionary/contemporary.
16 *The Call to Worship*, November 10, 1994.

Church outside Chicago and Community Church of Joy in Phoenix. Both of those churches had experienced significant growth by building congregational life around a culture of contemporary praise worship.

In the fall of 1996, the Celebration Team decided to develop specific plans for a contemporary praise worship service that would begin sometime in early 1997. People filled the Social Hall on November 12, 1996, for an evening of conversation with the Celebration Team about contemporary worship at Wyatt Park.[17] Two weeks later, the Administrative Cabinet approved a detailed plan, including a new worship schedule that would begin on February 2, 1997: informal traditional worship at 8:00 a.m., contemporary praise worship at 9:00 a.m., Sunday school at 10:00 a.m., and formal traditional worship at 11:00 a.m.[18] When the contemporary service started on February 2, Wyatt Park became the second established, denominational church in St. Joseph to offer the new style of worship (two independent, nondenominational churches also offered praise worship at that time).

In a break with custom among denominational churches, it was decided that Senior Pastor Gene Mockabee would serve as teaching pastor for the two traditional services each week, and I, as Associate Pastor, would serve as teaching pastor for the contemporary service.[19] We would both participate in all services, but each of us would also prepare a sermon every week. Such an arrangement was uncommon but not unheard of. On February 2, 1997, the first message (sermon) during a contemporary service at Wyatt Park was titled "Color Outside the Lines," and it focused on proclaiming the unchanging gospel in a new way. For the most part, the new style of worship was well received, but as with any significant change, there were some who did not like it and said so. Still, a new style of worship had begun at Wyatt Park, and some of those who were critical at the beginning became regular worshippers in the contemporary service later on.

---

17 *The Call to Worship*, October 31, 1996.

18 *The Call to Worship*, November 29, 1996.

19 As noted in the Introduction, I have made the stylistic choice to write in the first person when referring to myself.

During the late 1990s and early 2000s, the musicians who led weekly worship—the Praise Team—were frequently invited to take their music on the road. They performed at churches in Rosendale, Savannah, King City, Bolckow, and Bethany. In July 2000, they performed for a national gathering of Disciples of Christ men in Des Moines, Iowa. They were on the City Stage during St. Joseph's Trails West! Festival multiple times. In 2004 and again in 2005, they joined with musicians from other churches for Praise in the Park, held at the Krug Park amphitheater.

A special Fifth Friday Praise Service was held on the evening of March 30, 2001, during which time the Praise Team recorded its first (and to date only) CD.[20] Unlike most recordings by local church music teams, none of the CD was recorded in a studio. Instead, the recording was done live, before a capacity crowd in the sanctuary. Fifteen contemporary praise songs were recorded straight through, and the CD entitled "A Celebration of Praise" was released several weeks later.

Later that same year, a second contemporary praise service began at 5:00 p.m. on Saturday, October 13, 2001.[21] Although common in Roman Catholic congregations, Saturday services are rare among Protestants. The Saturday service was launched in response to both a need and an opportunity. Overcrowding during the 9:00 a.m. service resulted in the need for a second contemporary-praise-style service. At the same time, the cultural trend toward business-as-usual twenty-four hours per day, seven days per week created an opportunity to reach people who could not, or would not, worship on Sundays. Since its beginning, the 5:00 p.m. Saturday service has had average attendance of fifty to seventy people, so while it is smaller than the Sunday services, it is large enough to be viable. Twenty years after the first contemporary worship service, 75–80 percent of the people who worship at Wyatt Park on any given weekend choose one of the two praise-style services.[22]

---

20 Cabinet minutes, February 19, 2001.
21 *The Call to Worship*, September 26, 2001.
22 As of January 2017.

LEADING THE MUSIC

Countless singers have filled the ranks of choirs and Praise Teams through-out the years and have been accompanied by gifted instrumentalists. All of those musicians were guided by directors. From the beginning, music directors and some instrumentalists, especially organists, have been hired as part of the church staff. Most have been part-time, and some have remained in their positions for many years. Four of the longest tenured are briefly profiled below.

Emma Watts began her work as Choir Director in May 1918, when she was chosen to direct the sanctuary choir, and she held that position for four-teen years. In the fall of 1948, she again became a Choir Director but that time with a children's choir.

The Junior Choir (photo is dated 1948) grew rapidly, and within two years, a second choir was formed. The Carolers choir was open to elementary-age children, and the Clef choir was for Junior High youth. The impact of Emma Watts's ministry was described in *The Call to Worship:*

It is estimated that upwards of 1,000 different boys and girls have sung in her choirs through the years. In the winter of 1950, the Junior Choir program was expanded to a two choir program and the

Carolers Choir and the Clef Choir came into being. Both choirs sing in the morning services every Sunday.[23]

Emma Watts retired in 1961, and more than four hundred people attended a reception celebrating her many years of service to the church. She died in April 1966.

Thurley Lefler became the church organist in 1934 and remained in that position for eighteen years. She resigned in 1952 to go to First Christian Church downtown.[24] During her tenure an assistant organist was also hired, but with the unusual provision "that they pay the church 75 cents to $1 per hour for the privilege of practicing on the organ."[25] Despite the move to First Christian, Ms. Lefler stayed in contact with Wyatt Park and returned to play the organ for a special concert with the St. Joseph Symphony on March 1, 1964.[26] She remained at First Christian Church until her death in 2001.

Darren Verbick joined the music staff as organist in 1988 and continued in that role for twenty-five years until his retirement in 2013. He was named Music Director in 1996, and he also remained in that role until his retirement.[27] As Music Director, he directed the Chancel Choir; served during interim periods as Praise Team Leader; directed a bell choir, cantatas, and the music for special worship services, the Wyatt Park Windz (the congregation's concert band); and guided Wyatt Park's productions of two musicals: *Joseph and the Amazing Technicolor Dreamcoat* and *Godspell*. His June 2013 retirement coincided with the celebration of Wyatt Park's 125th anniversary, and the weekend culminated with the presentation of *My Utmost for His Highest*, a composition based on the classic Oswald Chambers daily devotional of the same name.[28]

Mark Pennington grew up in Buchanan County, and after several years singing with nationally known artists in musicals and on concert tours, he

---

23 *The Call to Worship*, January 7, 1959.

24 *The Call to Worship*, January 10, 1952.

25 Board minutes, November 13, 1950.

26 *The Call to Worship*, February 27, 1964.

27 *The Call to Worship*, January 4, 1996.

28 *The Call to Worship*, June 24, 2013.

returned to St. Joseph in 1996. Seven years later, in April 2003, he joined the Wyatt Park music staff as Praise Team Leader.[29] He continued in that role for ten years and then became Worship Director following the retirement of Darren Verbick in 2013. Equally at home with both praise and traditional style worship, he currently leads all of Wyatt Park's worship arts.

Other music directors and accompanists who served in those positions for at least five years include:

Charles Peters—Choir Director, 1935–1940
Katherine Moore—Director of Music, 1946–1951
Dr. Floyd Yurth—Assistant Organist, 1946–1948 and Organist 1971–1975
Lillian Cook—Pianist (children's choirs), 1948–1967
Byron Myers—Choir Director, 1959–1980 (He held multiple positions during those years, including Associate Pastor, and is profiled in chapter 8.)
Virginia Clay—Children's Choir Director, 1961–1967
Judy West—Organist, 1978–1986
Jeff Nolte—Choir Director, 1987–1994[30]

YOUTH-LED WORSHIP

Most weekends, worship services are led by the pastors and the musicians discussed above. Once in a while though, at least once a year, church youth lead worship. Youth-led worship was first mentioned in *The Call to Worship* in 1952, and it came at the conclusion of National Youth Week, observed by Christian Churches across the country. That first youth-led service did not deviate from the usual worship order. Rev. Tom Toler delivered the sermon, and high-school youth handled other elements of both Sunday morning

---

29 *The Call to Worship*, March 12, 2003.

30 The names, titles, and dates are drawn from history brochures, church directories, board and cabinet minutes, and worship bulletins.

services.[31] By the mid-1950s, the youth were handling all worship elements, including the sermons. Newsletter descriptions of those worship services indicate little change from the usual order or *feel* of worship. For example, a 1961 newsletter column by Rev. Clayton Potter commended the nearly 150 young people who helped lead worship services the previous weekend. He wrote, "They did so with reverence and dignity and poise."[32]

As already noted, reverence is a matter of the heart, and one can still be reverent while lacking some of what was considered "dignity and poise" during worship in years gone by. Changing cultural tastes influenced the conduct of youth-led worship services, just as they influenced worship in general. Beginning in the late 1960s, youth-led worship services came to include alternative ways to present the message, as dialogues and skits replaced the more standard sermon. Music also evolved, something that was especially true at Wyatt Park after the formation of the New Generation Singers. And, almost without fail, the order of worship would be different during youth-led services. Those new and different worship experiences were brought about because "Our youth are creative, imaginative, and untiring."[33] Periodic youth-led services are still a part of the worship routine at Wyatt Park, and the youth are still creative and imaginative and untiring.

AND...ACTION!

Drama is an art form that is older than Christianity itself. In the West, costumed actors and actresses telling a story on stage or screen is rooted in the ancient Greek and Roman theater, as long ago as the sixth century BCE. Theater arts have a mixed history in the Christian church. During some historical periods, acting on stage was seen as something Christians should avoid, and in some cultures and church traditions, that is still true today. At other times though, drama has been embraced by the church as an effective way to tell the story of Jesus and his people. With the rise of contemporary praise worship in the 1990s, drama, especially in the form of short skits, has

---

31 *The Call to Worship*, January 31, 1952.
32 *The Call to Worship*, February 2, 1961.
33 *The Call to Worship*, October 25, 1973.

experienced resurgence in congregational worship. At Wyatt Park, that resurgence began in the 1940s. It started, at least in an organized way, with this 1941 worship bulletin announcement:

> Miss Ruth Miller is asking all those interested in forming a DRAMATIC CLUB to come to the Homebuilders Room [Sunday-School class] Monday evening at 7:30. We need a serious minded group that will be interested in producing several outstanding one-act religious plays each year.[34]

Interest must have been considerable because by July there was a dramatic club; it was ready to stage a production, and it had a name, the Masquers. The name is rooted in the term "masque," used for a type of play that was especially popular in the sixteenth and seventeenth centuries.[35] The group's first production was a comedy, *Squaring It with the Boss*, presented in the Social Hall on July 23. A worship bulletin item about the upcoming play noted as follows: "Following the play, a free-will offering will be taken to help 'The Masquers' purchase needed stage equipment for the coming season's religious productions."[36] Those "religious productions" were often a part of worship and continued on a regular basis in the years that followed. Especially frequent were productions surrounding the stories of Jesus' birth at Christmas and of his death and resurrection at Easter.

In 1962, the Masquers offered classes for people interested in helping with productions. Classes were offered in "Costuming, Theatrical Makeup, Play Blocking, and Stage Management."[37] The Masquers presented productions at least throughout the 1960s.[38]

---

34 Worship Bulletin, May 25, 1941.

35 *Merriam-Webster Dictionary*, accessed online January 16, 2017, https://www.merriam-webster.com/dictionary/masque.

36 "News Sheet," dated July 23, 1941, filed with 1941–1942 worship bulletins.

37 *The Call to Worship*, May 24, 1962.

38 It is not known when the Masquers disbanded, but the last time the group was mentioned in *The Call to Worship* was a February 1969 announcement that preparations were underway for a Good Friday presentation. *The Call to Worship*, February 27, 1969.

At least two Broadway musicals have been presented in the sanctuary, and although not a part of regular worship services, they each told elements of the Christian story. And both musicals were presented twice.

Godspell was first presented at Wyatt Park in May 1978 by a traveling troupe from Indiana, the Indiana Central University Players. *Godspell* mixes the retelling of some of Jesus' parables with contemporary music.[39] Almost thirty years later, in November 2006, actors, actresses, and musicians from Wyatt Park presented the musical three times over the course of a weekend.[40] They were experienced with such a production because many of those same people had been involved in another musical just a few years before.

Joseph and the Amazing Technicolor Dreamcoat was first presented in November 2002.[41] With music composed by Andrew Lloyd Weber, *Joseph* tells the story of the patriarch Joseph and his "coat of many colors," a story found in Genesis 37–50. Because tickets for the musical quickly sold out, *Joseph* was presented again the following year, but with twice as many performances.[42]

With the advent of contemporary praise worship in 1997, drama came to be used during worship services, often in conjunction with the message. Almost always in the form of short skits, the scripts initially came from outside sources, but later on I wrote the scripts, making it possible to directly link the skit and the message.

THE TIME, IT IS A CHANGIN'

Gathering each Sunday for worship has been a part of Wyatt Park's congregational life since its beginning in 1888. That has not changed. What *has* changed through the years is exactly *when* on Sunday those gatherings take place. For many decades in North America, the most popular time for worship was sometime around 11:00 a.m. No biblical mandate exists for such a time. Rather, worship at 11:00 a.m. was the product of an agrarian society,

---

39 *The Call to Worship*, May 11, 1978.
40 *The Call to Worship*, November 22, 2006.
41 *The Call to Worship*, November 20, 2002.
42 *The Call to Worship*, October 29, 2003.

and for farmers it fell midway between the times to milk the cows. That worked well for its time, but this is no longer a predominantly agrarian society, and worship times are, put simply, all over the clock face.

Although most people choose to worship on Sunday mornings, regular services have been offered at other times. From as early as the late 1920s, and continuing until 1946, Wyatt Park offered a weekly Sunday evening service.[43] Since 2001, a Saturday evening service has been offered. Even on Sunday mornings, there are options, and they have changed through the years.

Until 1946, there was one service on Sunday mornings. It was a late morning service, except during the summer. In those days before air-conditioning, the worship service was moved to an earlier time during the summer in order to escape the heat. Beginning in 1946, two services were offered on Sunday mornings, but the schedule returned to one early service during the hottest summer months.[44] Once the new air-conditioned sanctuary opened in 1957, the regular two-service worship schedule was maintained year-round.[45]

Since 1946, multiple worship services have been offered with one fourteen-year exception. There was only one Sunday morning service from 1972 until 1986, and during most of those years, it began at 10:30.[46] Offering two Sunday morning services resumed in 1986, and then in 1997, the contemporary praise service was added, meaning three services on Sunday mornings. The current schedule of two Sunday morning services, one at 9:15 and the other at 10:45, began in 2009. Multiple factors influence the scheduling of worship services, and high on the list of considerations is worship attendance trends.

EVERY NUMBER HAS A NAME

Congregational health can be measured in several different ways, and one of the easiest is worship attendance. All that is required is a head count, and

---

43 No record could be found indicating the worship schedule prior to March 1928.

44 *The Call to Worship*, October 10, 1946.

45 *The Call to Worship*, May 14, 1958.

46 *The Call to Worship*, August 31, 1972.

the attendance numbers matter because every one of those numbers has a name. There are other aspects of congregational life that can, and should, be measured: financial support, participation in classes and small groups, involvement in missions' ministries, and so forth. In the end, though, worship attendance is about people participating in the single most important element of congregational life—worship.

Interestingly, worship attendance was not regularly reported in the newsletter or meeting minutes until the 1950s. It was written about though. In 1948, Rev. Lawrence Bash lamented poor attendance at worship: "Last Sunday, Memorial Day, was a disaster. There were only 350 in the worship services (which was terrible!)." He went on to offer a prescription: "I know the cure. Nothing less, nothing more than a little more loyalty on the part of church members. Let's put first things first!"[47]

Regular worship attendance peaked in the mid-1950s with an average of 600–650 each weekend.[48] Even with the large number of worshippers, the need for regular worship attendance was frequently stressed in the newsletter. Consider this excerpt from a lengthy article in the first newsletter of 1957:

> Our attendance record is good, but it can be better. One reason for working for higher and higher attendance records is not just for the record's sake. It is because we believe that church attendance is vital to the growth of the Christian life. No person can grow toward Christ-likeness by voluntarily absenting himself from the worship and communion services of his church. It is in the fellowship of other Christians who are striving to follow the Master that we follow more closely.
>
> As we begin this new year of 1957, let one resolution be that insofar as we are able, every one of us will be in the worship services of our church and at the Lord's Table on every Sunday. Only a physical excuse (such as work, illness, etc.) should keep us away.

---

47 *The Call to Worship*, June 3, 1948.

48 By the mid-1950s, worship attendance numbers were regularly reported in *The Call to Worship*, a practice that continues to this day.

There are two rules we must follow if our church attendance is to be joyful and regular. The first is to remember that church-going, like so many other things in life, is a habit. It is much easier to keep on going to church than it is to start going to church.

What followed was discussion of a second rule having to do with regular worship attendance, and it related to one's thinking on Saturday. If thoughts of skipping worship the next day enter into people's minds on Saturday, chances are quite high that they will act on those thoughts come Sunday. The article concluded with this:

Our church membership now numbers approximately 1,300. There should be no less than 750 in church on Sunday morning on the average to match the present-day national average. Actually, we should do better than that. Remember: your presence is needed every Sunday morning at one of the two worship and communion services. You need it. Your church needs it.[49]

Worship attendance averaged about six hundred in the beginning of the 1960s, but the cultural turbulence of the decade impacted the church as well.

College campus unrest, the war in Vietnam, and the Civil Rights Movement all combined to make the 1960s a decade of incredible change in American culture. What had seemed to be cultural *norms* about God, country, family, and morality were increasingly rejected. Since many of those *norms* were rooted in the Judeo-Christian tradition, it is not surprising that the church and what it teaches were increasingly rejected as well. Rev. Bill Mallotte noted that trend in a 1971 newsletter article:

Since 1960, the number of persons attending public worship in the United States has been on a downward spiral. The Wyatt Park Christian Church is no exception. In 1960, we had an average of 611

---

49 *The Call to Worship*, January 2, 1957.

persons worshiping here each Sunday and there has been a gradual decline in consecutive years. Only time will tell if 1971 will continue the downward spiral or if we have "hit bottom" and will either level off or begin to increase.[50]

When Rev. Mallotte wrote that article, worship attendance averaged in the mid–three hundreds, and it has essentially remained at that level in the years since. Attendance dropped below three hundred for a few years in the 1980s and early 1990s and rose above four hundred for a few years in the early 2000s. Otherwise, weekly worship attendance at Wyatt Park has held steady. At this writing in 2017, a trend being noticed across the country is not so much that fewer people are worshiping, but that people are worshiping *less often*. Either way, the pressure continues for most congregations in terms of worship attendance.

C AND E WORSHIP

"C and E Christians" is the term used for (and sometimes by) people who only attend worship twice a year: during Christmas and Easter. Regardless of whether one worships weekly or only twice a year, Christmas and Easter *are* special times for people of faith to gather together. "Christmas" and "Easter" are actually seasons in the Christian Church year and have been observed for centuries. The Christmas season begins on Christmas Day and continues for twelve days. The Easter season begins on Easter Sunday and continues for six weeks until the day of Pentecost. Throughout much of its history, Wyatt Park Christian Church has observed the season of Advent, a four-week season of preparation before Christmas. Since the early 2000s, the congregation has also observed Lent, a six-week season of preparation before Easter. In addition to the regular schedule of worship services, seasons surrounding Christmas and Easter often include additional times of worship. That is especially true during Holy Week, the week leading up to Easter Sunday.

---

50 *The Call to Worship*, March 11, 1971.

The season of Lent begins on Ash Wednesday, a day that has been observed for centuries in Roman Catholic and some Protestant churches. Ash Wednesday was first observed at Wyatt Park in 2015 when the practice of an annual service began. During the Ash Wednesday service, ashes in the shape of a cross are placed on the foreheads of worshippers. Ashes symbolize the sin that stains each person and provide a visual reminder of the need for salvation in Jesus Christ. The service is intended to set the tone for Lent by encouraging a spirit of repentance and a desire for growth in devotion to Jesus.

Cantatas are a regular feature of special worship services surrounding Christmas and Easter. Cantatas are long-form compositions that typically include multiple songs and narration that is biblically based and/or consists of direct quotes from scripture. Presentation of cantatas at Wyatt Park goes back to at least the 1920s. Newspaper articles from 1926 and 1928 describe Easter cantatas telling the story of the death and resurrection of Jesus.[51] The cantatas have been presented by Wyatt Park vocalists, joined on occasion by singers from other churches.

Gathering together for the Lord's Supper is a part of weekly worship at Wyatt Park, and throughout most of its history, there has also been a special remembrance of the Lord's Supper on the Thursday of Holy Week, known as Maundy Thursday. "Maundy" is rooted in a Latin word that is connected with Jesus's command to his disciples the night he shared that last meal with them: "A new commandment I give to you, that you love one another: just as I have loved you, you also are to love one another" (John 13:34). Maundy Thursday worship is always centered on the act of partaking of the bread and the cup, the Lord's Supper. Over the years, it has also included silence, cantatas, drama, or a mixture of scripture readings and music.

Good Friday is the day during Holy Week when Christ's death on the cross is the focus. Although not as frequent as Maundy Thursday services, Good Friday has been observed in different ways throughout the years: cantatas, drama, silence, darkness, and so forth. In the early 2000s, Good

---

51 *St. Joseph News-Press*, 1926 and 1928. Exact dates are unknown. The articles are included in the 1887–1948 historical scrapbook.

Friday worship included Taize-style music and the Stations of the Cross.[52] Most recently, Good Friday has marked the start of a twenty-four-hour prayer vigil, beginning at 3:00 p.m. on Good Friday, the time of day that scripture says Jesus died on the cross. The vigil continues until 3:00 p.m. on Saturday. During the entire time, congregation members are at the church in prayer.

Holy Week builds to a climax on Easter Sunday when the resurrection of Jesus is celebrated. On Easter Sunday, we celebrate the amazing discovery that was made on a Sunday morning some two thousand years ago. The tomb in which Jesus was buried was found-empty, and encounters with the risen Lord began shortly thereafter. Many times through the congregation's history, Wyatt Park folk have gathered at sunrise on Easter Sunday to celebrate the resurrection of Jesus. In a 1949 newsletter, board chairman Ralph Sawyer wrote about the beauty of worshiping at sunrise:

> We especially urge you to attend the Sunrise service. There is something about that service that inspires you more than any other service. Somehow, we seem to draw just a little closer to God. In the early morning hour, when the world begins to awaken, the Resurrection seems more real.[53]

Most years, sunrise services have been held in the sanctuary, but occasionally the service moved outside. Bartlett Park, just a few blocks from the church, was the location for multiple sunrise services. In 1993, the sunrise service was held atop Wyeth Hill, overlooking the Missouri River just north of downtown.

Regular worship services on Easter Sunday are celebratory. Overflow crowds are common as are decorations and extra music. Some Easter Sundays

---

52 Taize-style music consists of simple, repetitive, meditative chants. It was developed at an ecumenical monastery in Taize, France, and has become quite popular around the world. The Stations of the Cross is usually associated with the Roman Catholic Church, although many Protestants use it as a means of devotion around the time of Easter. There are fourteen "stations," images depicting scenes of the final hours of Jesus's life and then immediately after his death.

53 *The Call to Worship*, April 14, 1949.

have featured dramas. Many have included baptisms. It is a joyful time as the congregation gathers to celebrate the resurrection of Jesus Christ.

Several months after Easter, on December 25, Christians celebrate the birth of Jesus. Most years, Christmas Day is not a day of worship at Wyatt Park because it usually falls on a day other than Sunday. So the days and weeks leading up to Christmas Day are times for special music programs, worship services, and pageants. Little is known about Christmas festivities in the earliest years, but by the early 1940s, annual Christmas pageants were held, typically on the Sunday evening before Christmas. Several pageants featured the Masquers, the drama troupe, and they always included special music by soloists, small groups, and choirs. A worship bulletin for the 1943 Christmas pageant is illustrative. It lists nine pieces of music shared by soloists or choirs, three congregational hymns, four scenes depicted by costumed actors, prayers, and an offering.[54]

In what might be considered a precursor of today's Christmas Tableau drive-through living nativity (see chapter 5), by 1945 the term "Living Pictures" was regularly used in reference to the role of those in costume during the pageants. "Living Pictures" continued to be a part of Christmas pageants until at least the early 1960s. This photo from 1961 appeared on the newsletter cover the following year, promoting the upcoming "Living Pictures" pageant on Sunday evening, December 23.[55]

Christmas Eve worship is an important part of the season for most families in the congregation, but it was not always that way. Worship on Christmas Eve was first

---

54 Worship bulletin, Christmas pageant, December 19, 1943.

55 *The Call to Worship*, December 20, 1962. The picture is captioned as follows: "Shown are, from left to right, Mr. and Mrs. W. Bart McAnnich and baby, Mr. Paul Clay, Mr. Richard Rochambeau, and Mr. Robert Powell."

introduced in 1955, and with a surprising lack of enthusiasm. That first Christmas Eve service was held at 11:30 p.m., December 24, 1955. Described as a service of communion, the service was called "Christmas Eve Service of the Cradle and the Grail." It was planned to be about forty-five minutes in length and devotional in nature. Because of concern about possible intrusion into traditional family gatherings, the article describing the new service includes this curious sentence: "We are not highly promoting attendance for this service, but we do cordially invite everyone who finds it possible to do so, to attend."[56] Three hundred fifty-two people attended, more than double what worship planners had anticipated. Not surprisingly, Christmas Eve worship has been an annual highlight at Wyatt Park every year since.[57]

For many years there was just one Christmas Eve service, typically at 11:00 p.m. That changed in 1983 with the addition of an early Family Service at 6:00 p.m., geared toward families with young children.[58] One feature of the Family Service was reminiscent of the Christmas pageants of years gone by as people in costume depicted a live nativity scene. Beginning in 1997, the early Christmas Eve service offered contemporary praise music, and attendance at that service grew significantly. By 2005, a third Christmas Eve service was added to the schedule, and it remains so today: contemporary praise Christmas Eve services at 5:00 p.m. and 7:00 p.m. and a more traditional service at 11:00 p.m. All of the services include carols, scripture, prayers, communion, and candlelight.[59]

SPECIAL SERVICES

Worship at Wyatt Park occurs each weekend, and there are almost always additional services around Christmas and Easter. Once in a while, special worship services are held, and the reasons behind them are many. While there were likely special services in prior years, the first documented mention of one

56 *The Call to Worship*, December 7, 1955.
57 *The Call to Worship*, December 28, 1955.
58 *The Call to Worship*, December 1, 1983.
59 *The Call to Worship*, December 7, 2005.

was in 1916 when the Wyatt Park congregation joined with the congregation of Huffman Memorial Church for a Thanksgiving service.[60] Although not held annually, there were many times in subsequent years when the Wyatt Park congregation joined with neighboring congregations for Thanksgiving services.

Revivals were held in the early years, usually lasting for a week with worship each evening. Guest preachers were common, but there were some years when Wyatt Park's pastor served as the revival preacher.

Multiple celebrations of the congregation's anniversary have taken place, each including special worship services. In 1938, Wyatt Park's fiftieth anniversary was marked by special worship services, children's programming, a pageant, and a "tea" sponsored by the Women's Council.[61] Twenty-five years later, the congregation observed its seventy-fifth anniversary in 1963, and a special afternoon worship service was the primary event.[62] A month-long celebration was held in October 1988 to mark the congregation's one-hundredth anniversary. Worship during each of the first four Sundays of the month focused on a different twenty-five-year segment of the congregation's history.[63] Former pastor Dr. Gene Mockabee and Rev. Kyle Maxwell, a "Timothy" of Wyatt Park, led morning worship services in June 2013 as the congregation observed its 125th anniversary. As noted above, that celebration culminated with an evening presentation of the cantata, *My Utmost for His Highest.*[64]

World events have prompted special worship services, especially during wartime. There were special times of worship, usually prayer services, during World War I, World War II, and the Korean War. About one hundred people gathered on short notice for a 10:00 p.m. prayer service at the height of the Cuban Missile Crisis in 1962.[65] On September 11, 2001, minutes after the terrorist attacks in New York and Washington, Wyatt Park ministry staff

---

60 Board minutes, November 6, 1916.

61 *St. Joseph News-Press*, 1938. Exact date is unknown.

62 *The Call to Worship*, October 3, 1963.

63 *The Call to Worship*, September 8, 1988.

64 *The Call to Worship*, June 24, 2013.

65 *The Call to Worship*, November 1, 1962.

used multiple means of communication to invite other pastors in St. Joseph to gather for the purpose of organizing a community-wide prayer service. By 11:00 a.m. more than sixty pastors were present in the Wyatt Park sanctuary. A small group was selected to work out details, and that evening, a crowd estimated at twenty-five hundred gathered at Missouri Western State University for a prayer service led by pastors from many area churches. Prayers were offered for victims, first responders, government leaders, and even the perpetrators that God would somehow turn them in a new direction.[66]

Worship on the Air

During the middle part of the twentieth century, Wyatt Park Christian Church had a radio ministry. Worship services themselves were not broadcast, but at different times over a span of nearly twenty years, Wyatt Park pastors shared devotional messages intended to help people worship at home. Their messages were aired at different times of the day and night and were generally under fifteen minutes in length.

Rev. Lawrence Bash was the first Wyatt Park pastor to regularly appear on the radio. He did a series of hymn interpretations in 1946 on KRES Radio (1230 AM).[67] Throughout 1947, Rev. Bash presented a fifteen-minute devotion every Saturday on KFEQ Radio (680 AM).[68] His series of broadcasts was titled *The Call to Worship*. At least two of his broadcast manuscripts have survived to today. "The Treasures of the Snow" was broadcast on January 4, 1947. He used the beauty of the snowflake as a way to point people to the majesty of God. One month later, on February 1, 1947, he broadcast "What Are You Looking For?" In that broadcast, he encouraged listeners to consider what they seek and to seek good things.[69]

---

66 *St. Joseph News-Press*, September 12, 2001.

67 Worship bulletin, September 1946.

68 *The Call to Worship*, December 26, 1946, and January 1, 1948.

69 The manuscripts of Rev. Bash's two broadcasts are included in the 1887–1948 historical scrapbook.

Associate Pastor Merwin Coad did a daily broadcast on KRES through-out 1948–1949. It was devotional in nature, and his messages were presented through poetry and music.[70] Rev. Tom Toler presented a series of daily devotions on KRES in 1953.[71] During the season of Lent in 1962, Rev. Tommie Bouchard was featured on a daily fifteen-minute program on KKJO (1550 AM). "A Faith to Live By" aired each morning at 7:05 for a period of six weeks. It was intended to reach shut-ins and "the large segment of our population who are not actively related to the churches of our city." Its format included "thoughts for the day, commentary, and good music."[72] "A Faith to Live By" continued through April 20, 1962, and its conclusion brought to a close nearly twenty years of over-the-air broadcast ministry by Wyatt Park Christian Church.

BROADCASTING—TWENTY-FIRST-CENTURY STYLE

Radio was a useful way to reach people in the twentieth century. In the twenty-first century, the Internet has made it possible to reach people in greater numbers, anywhere in the world. In the past, a local congregation might purchase airtime on a local radio station and use it to broadcast a worship service or some other type of programming (e.g., what was described in the previous section). However the airtime was used, the broadcast would be on a particular station at a particular time, and the potential audience would be limited to the geographic area covered by the radio station's signal. With the advent of the Internet, a worship service can be streamed live or recorded, uploaded to a website, and then accessed at any time from any location that has access to the World Wide Web.

Wyatt Park Christian Church began uploading sermon audio files to the congregation's website in January 2013. Internet tracking tools show that although the audio files are most often accessed by people within driving distance of the church, they are also accessed by people across the United States

---

70 *The Call to Worship*, September 30, 1948, and December 9, 1948.

71 *The Call to Worship*, June 11, 1953.

72 *The Call to Worship*, February 22, 1962.

and in a few foreign countries. Cameras were installed in the sanctuary in early 2017 making it possible to stream live and upload video files of worship services, meaning people anywhere in the world may watch worship at Wyatt Park on a computer, tablet, or mobile device.

So twenty-first-century worship at Wyatt Park features a message, communion, and music led by a praise band. It is then uploaded to the Internet and made available around the world. Worship services look and feel different today than in the summer of 1888 when Wyatt Park Christian Church was organized, but sermons are still grounded in the Bible; there are still prayers and a weekly gathering around the communion table, and the Good News of the gospel of Jesus Christ is still proclaimed. Methods may change, but the message does not.

CHAPTER 4

Gathered to Grow

—

You shall love the LORD your God with all your heart and
with all your soul and with all your might. And these words
that I command you today shall be on your heart. You shall
teach them diligently to your children, and shall talk of them
when you sit in your house, and when you walk by the way,
and when you lie down, and when you rise. (Deut. 6:5–7)

FOR MOST CHRISTIANS WHO GREW up in the church during the twentieth century, the term "Christian education" brings to mind another term, "Sunday
School." Sunday-School classes were generally structured to resemble classes
in public or private schools, and there was a reason for that. When Sunday
Schools first began, they truly were *schools*, offering education to children who
spent the rest of the week working in factories. Sunday Schools began in Great
Britain in the 1780s when the Industrial Revolution was well underway.

Workdays for children routinely exceeded twelve hours, and the work-
week included Saturdays. Therefore, Sunday was the only day available to
offer children some education that would hopefully lift them out of a life
of poverty and illiteracy. An English Anglican named Robert Raikes is considered the father of what became known as the Sunday School Movement.
Denominations quickly embraced the idea, and it soon spread to North
America. Religious education was an important part of the curriculum, and
the Bible was a primary textbook for learning to read. Children learned to

write by copying passages from the Bible. Christian morality and values were also taught.

By the late 1800s, government-run schools were operating, and children transitioned from factory work to getting an education. From that point on, children learned to read and write during the week, and Sunday-School curriculum was limited to religious education.

As noted in chapter 1, Wyatt Park Christian Church began as a Sunday-School class in the summer of 1888. Not surprisingly, Christian education, especially in the form of Sunday School, has been an important part of the congregation's life ever since.

Nothing has been found to indicate how many classrooms were in the original building at Twenty-Seventh and Olive. Regardless of the number of rooms, Sunday-School attendance in the early years of the twentieth century typically ranged from 75 to 125 students. Attendance varied then, just as it does today. Many of the class records also noted how many students brought Bibles, how many were on time, and the amount received in the class offering.[1] By 1915, the church board concluded that a Religious Education Committee was needed to coordinate the Sunday-School program.[2] When Wyatt Park Christian Church marked its fiftieth anniversary in 1938, Sunday-School enrollment exceeded four hundred. Fred Roach was the Sunday-School Superintendent, and there were seven departmental superintendents: Adult, Junior, Young People, Primary, Beginners, Nursery, and Cradle Roll.[3] By 1940, Sunday-School enrollment surpassed six hundred, and more than two dozen men and women served as teachers.[4]

Teaching the teachers became an important part of the congregation's ministry in the mid-1950s. Wyatt Park Christian Church joined with other Christian Churches in northwest Missouri for an Observation School in 1953. Over the course of a weekend, teachers (and potential future teachers) observed as "some of the best children's teachers in our churches" taught

1 Sunday-school attendance books, 1913–1924.
2 Board minutes, June 7, 1915.
3 *Yearbook*, Wyatt Park Christian Church, 1938.
4 *Yearbook*, Wyatt Park Christian Church, 1940.

different age groups. After observing the teaching for an hour, teachers (and potential teachers) had an extended opportunity to visit with the leaders they had just observed. Sixty-five people attended, forty of them from Wyatt Park.[5] Two years later, teacher training was offered on a larger scale, a weeklong State Laboratory Training School. Intended for church staff and volunteer teachers, people from throughout northwest Missouri were invited. It was rigorous, with sessions lasting several hours each day, and its description included this:

Being guided by the school's leaders you will learn by doing: by planning a session, telling a story or guiding children in useful activities. There will be evaluation periods, library hours, creative activities, and a leadership training course.[6]

Twenty-one people from Wyatt Park participated in the school.[7]

In October 1962, considerable space in *The Call to Worship* was devoted to the importance of Christian education for children and youth. A front-page article noted that more than four hundred children and youth participated in youth groups and other related activities during a one-week period in October. Another full-page article described needs and dreams for those ministries. While some of the article dealt with facility needs, most of it focused on programming, and it began with a reminder about the point of it all:

This must be taken seriously when we realize that the cornerstone of the next generation is being laid today by the manner in which we provide for the spiritual development of our children and youth.[8]

Less than two months later, Rev. Tommie Bouchard noted an estimate that by 1965, one-half of the population in the United States would be under the age of twenty-five. He wrote that the church should take note and face the

---

5 *The Call to Worship*, November 12, 1953, and December 10, 1953.
6 *The Call to Worship*, April 21, 1955.
7 *The Call to Worship*, May 19, 1955.
8 *The Call to Worship*, October 18, 1962.

challenge of reaching these new generations for Christ. He wrote that "No one is born a Christian," and therefore people must learn the faith "under the careful and steadfast guidance of others who are committed to Christ."[9] His statement is as true today as it was more than fifty years ago.

As noted in the previous chapter, by 1971, worship attendance had declined considerably from its peak in the 1950s. A similar decline was experienced in the congregation's Christian education programming, especially Sunday School. Midway through 1971, a report titled "Program 1970–71" was shared with the congregation. It summarized the previous program year in multiple ministry areas, including Christian education, and it was quite candid about strengths and weaknesses. Although the facility was seen as a strength, participation in classes and groups was described as only "fair." Weaknesses included a lack of volunteers, little use of what was described as a "very good" church library, and the report noted, "Little Christian education taking place in youth and adult levels. Adult: fellowship only, little education."[10] It recommended a concentrated effort on "basics" classes and leadership development.

By 1980, class attendance had declined enough that the board approved a proposal from the Property Department to not use the third floor for three months during the winter. Two goals were given: (1) use the facility more efficiently and (2) save on heating costs.[11] There is no indication that the experiment extended beyond the three-month period or that it was repeated in subsequent years.

Through the 1990s and into the mid-2000s, Sunday-School attendance averaged 150–200 per week, but a trend became increasingly evident, resulting in an altered view of Christian education. For most of its history, Christian education at Wyatt Park Christian Church primarily took place on Sunday morning as classes met for Sunday School. Groups for children, youth, and adults met at times other than Sunday mornings certainly, but participation in those groups was typically *in addition to* attending Sunday School. A few

9 *The Call to Worship*, November 8, 1962.

10 Program 1970–1971, filed with board minutes, July 1970–June 1971.

11 *The Call to Worship*, December 24, 1980.

years into the twenty-first century, it became evident that more and more people were gathering at times other than Sunday morning, and that those gatherings were taking the place of Sunday School. While Christian education for all ages continues to be offered on Sunday mornings, participation is greater in classes and small groups that meet at other times and often at locations outside the church building. In addition, the terminology has changed a bit with Christian education offerings now coming under the heading of "discipleship groups." That term is rooted in the Great Commission in Matthew 28 wherein Jesus said to his disciples:

> Go therefore and make disciples of all nations, baptizing them in the name of the Father and of the Son and of the Holy Spirit, teaching them to obey all that I have commanded you. And behold, I am with you always, to the end of the age. (Matt. 28:19-20)

Wyatt Park Christian Church has a long history of adapting to changing circumstances, and adapting to changing preferences about the timing and locale of Christian education is but one illustration.

CLASSES AND SMALL GROUPS

Weekly worship, concerts, and fellowship dinners bring people together in large numbers. When it comes to Christian education, small numbers work best, so church members have organized themselves into classes and small groups since the congregation's beginning in 1888. Those classes and groups all started with enthusiasm and good intentions, but many of them lasted only a short time. Still, some classes managed to span multiple decades. What follows are descriptions of some of the longest-running classes for which information is available.

The Home Builders Class was organized in 1925 and existed for nearly sixty years. Active throughout its history, the class was taught by H. L. Dannen in the early years and then by Leland Becraft. Ralph Sawyer and Glen Gerard are listed as teachers in the 1960s. The names of other teachers are unknown.

For many years, it was the largest adult Sunday-School class, with so many members that it sometimes met in the Social Hall. In addition to regular class meetings on Sunday mornings, the class gathered once a month for a social event. By 1983, the class had merged with the Capp-tivators Class.[12]

The Capp-tivators Class was organized in 1933 with Theresa Capp serving as the first teacher. It continued for nearly seventy years. By 1938, the class had grown to seventy-five members (pictured in photo above). Health problems prompted a change in leadership, and Ralph Sawyer assumed the role of teacher in the mid-1940s. Theresa Capp died in 1949, and her final years were recalled in *The Call to Worship*:

> The qualities of cheerfulness and courage which marked the last years of Miss Capp's life will long be remembered by all who knew her. These were years of severe suffering and tragedy, but they never destroyed her faith.[13]

Class members gathered monthly for social and/or service events, and they often held fund raisers to benefit a project or program within the church. Summertime breakfasts at Bartlett Park were popular fund raisers for several years. By 1983, the Homebuilder's Class and the Capp-tivator's Class had merged, and it was listed as a combined class, but by the 1990s, it was known simply as the Capp-tivator's Class. A complete listing of teachers has

---

12 *Yearbook*, Wyatt Park Christian Church, 1938; *Yearbook*, Wyatt Park Christian Church, 1948; *Program / Calendar*, Wyatt Park Christian Church, 1961–1962, 1963–1964, 1964–1965.

13 *The Call to Worship*, October 6, 1949.

not been found, but among the instructors were Ralph Sawyer, Fred Roach, and Darryle Bartlett. Lila Redmon was listed as the teacher in 2002, the last year the Capp-tivator's Class was mentioned in *The Call to Worship*.[14]

The Business Women's Class formed in the 1940s and continued for forty years, until at least 1983. In a 1946 brochure, the class was described as being "for the young business women of the church." Interestingly, in that brochure it is listed as "The Business Girls' Class," and it appears to have been listed that way only once.[15] In addition to Sunday mornings, class members gathered at least once a month for social and/or service activities. Some of the teachers included Mrs. L. R. Ricklefs, Mildred Bringmen, and Mrs. Allan Neale. The class was last listed in 1983.[16]

There was talk in 1936 about the need for a new Sunday-School class for young married couples. Just over a year later, near the end of 1937, the 50-50 Class was organized, and it continued for more than seventy-five years. The name "50-50" was deemed appropriate for young couples sharing (50-50) in the tasks of family, home, and community life. By 1940, the class included eighteen married couples, and during the 1950s and 1960s, the class consistently had membership of 160–170. In addition to Sunday School, the 50-50 Class also held monthly social and/or service activities throughout much of its history. History was important to the class—Wyatt Park's history, and the history of the class itself. For many years, the class used an important piece of the congregation's history, the pulpit that was in the first sanctuary at Twenty-Seventh and Olive and then in the second sanctuary at Twenty-Seventh and Mitchell. It served as the lectern from which numerous teachers led the class. The longest-tenured teacher was Chester "Smokey" Stover, who taught the class for twenty-one years, from 1952 until his death in 1973. On July 12, 1987, the 50-50 Class celebrated its fiftieth anniversary, and a highlight of the weekend came during morning worship when class

---

14 *The Call to Worship*, September 4, 2002. Also *Yearbook*, 1938; *Yearbook*, 1948; *Program / Calendar*, 1961–1962, 1964–1965, 1966–1967; *WPCC Program*, 1983.

15 Brochure, *The Program of the Wyatt Park Christian Church*, 1946

16 *WPCC Program*, 1983. Also *Yearbook*, 1948; Program / Calendar / Program, 1961–1962, 1964–1965, 1966–1967.

members—eighty-seven of them—sat together in the pews.[17] Age took a toll, and by the early 2000s the class had diminished in size, and by 2011 it was no longer self-sustaining. From then on, the few remaining class members met weekly with the Keystone Class, and in a very real way the life of both classes came full circle.

By 1946, there was agreement that the church needed a new class for younger married couples. In response, the 50-50 Class sanctioned and helped organize the Keystone Class, a class that continued for nearly seventy years.[18] The class grew quickly with Glenn Gerard as its first teacher.[19] Teachers in the years that followed included David Price and Ralph Sawyer, and then for many years, class members took turns leading discussions. Some Keystone Class members enjoyed theater arts, so the class occasionally presented plays. A three-act comedy, *Oh, Aunt Jerusha*, was presented in 1949. Admission was thirty-five cents for adults and ten cents for children.[20] Six years later, the class presented another three-act comedy, *Meet Sis Perkins*. Admission was still thirty-five cents for adults, but the cost for children increased to fifteen cents. Proceeds went toward the congregation's building fund.[21] Keystone Class members undertook an unusual, and apparently one-time, effort in 1956 to support the building fund, by operating a fireworks stand at Mitchell Avenue and the Belt Highway.[22] In the years that followed, members of the Keystone Class held leadership positions throughout the church, and the class remained very active into the early 2000s. Age took a toll, however, and attendance declined. As noted above, by 2011, the Keystone Class reunited with the group that helped organize it sixty-five years earlier, the 50-50 Class. In July 2015, longtime Keystone Class member Jeannetta Danford wrote an article for *The Call to Worship*, and it included these words:

---

17 Scrapbook, *50-50 Class History*, stored with other historical scrapbooks.

18 Ibid.

19 *Yearbook*, 1948.

20 *The Call to Worship*, April 28, 1949.

21 *The Call to Worship*, April 21, 1955.

22 *The Call to Worship*, June 13, 1956.

The Keystone and 50-50 Class members have reluctantly decided to lower the curtain on the long history of the combined classes. Due to age, normal illnesses, and the deaths of many valued members, the class has dwindled greatly in size the past few years. Both classes were dynamic during their long history. The Keystone Class began in the mid to late 1940s and the 50-50 Class some years prior to that. At those times, members were young married couples with small children. They crowded the classrooms on Sundays, most were actively engaged in leadership positions throughout the church, and all were active and raised their children in the church. Sadly, the natural condition of advancing years has left only a few faithful members to participate in the class. The time has come, and it is hoped that other, younger members will participate in classes that will give them the same foundation for their belief and family situations.[23]

The five classes described above had the longest histories, but other classes also gathered together over many years. Examples include the Koinonia (Christian fellowship) Class that began in 1958 and continued meeting until the mid-1970s. The Oikos Koinonia (house of fellowship) Class formed in the early 1980s. As of this writing (2017), the OK Class continues to meet weekly and is active in many areas of the congregation's life. The Friendship Class was organized in 1990 and met weekly until 2001. The Spiritual Growth Class formed in the early 1990s and met until early 2014. The Atrium Class formed in the mid-1990s and continues to meet weekly.[24] As has been the case throughout Wyatt Park's history, Sunday-School classes continue to form. Most recently, a new class for young married couples began in autumn of 2016. And then there are the gatherings at times other than Sunday mornings.

In a culture that is increasingly twenty-four-hours-a-day, seven-days-a-week, it has become necessary for local churches to offer worship and learning opportunities at different times and locales. Such was the motivation behind the start

---

23 *The Call to Worship*, July 28, 2015.

24 Documentation concerning these classes is limited. Some of the beginning and/or ending dates are estimated based on board meeting minutes and/or newsletter entries.

of the Saturday worship service discussed in chapter 3. While there have always been fellowship and study groups meeting at times other than Sunday morning at Wyatt Park, those offerings play a larger role in this new cultural setting. For many participants, those gatherings have taken the place of Christian education on Sunday mornings. At present, the following adult groups meet weekly: Tuesday morning women's study group; Tuesday evening young adults study group; Monday afternoon college student study group; Wednesday evening - multiple study groups for adults; and Thursday morning men's study group. Multiple discipleship groups for children and youth meet on Wednesday evenings.

Ministry to Children

Many things have changed around Wyatt Park since 1888, but some things have remained the same. As an example of the latter, consider the suggestion made during a board meeting that some board members be present with the children's group on Sunday mornings "and help to keep order among the boys who behave badly." Such a statement would be possible most anytime, and not just about young boys, but in this case the recommendation was made in 1918.[25] Handing down the faith to children was commanded by God when He gave the law to the Israelites at Mount Sinai (Deut. 6:5–7), and it has been

an important part of life in faith communities ever since. And it is never dull.

Through the decades, children have most often been grouped together by age (above photo).[26] In 1936, for example, there were four children's classes: Nursery, Beginners, Junior, and

---

25 Board minutes, July 1, 1918.

26 The 1959 photo shows one of the children's classes with teacher Laura Ream.

Primary. A newsletter page devoted to children's classes noted that eighty-six children had been in attendance the previous Sunday.[27] Age group configurations have changed over the years as have class formats and curriculums. One constant has been, and still is, the need for adults who will teach the children. For many of those adults, working with children in the church is not just a job to be done by a volunteer. It is a calling from God. One such teacher was Mabel Ellis who started teaching kindergarten boys and girls in 1927. She served in that capacity for the next thirty-three years, but she did not "retire" in February 1960. Rather, she moved into a larger role as Superintendent of Children's Work.[28] Rev. Clayton Potter noted in his newsletter column that she always understood that the children not only listened to her words, but they also watched her actions; "therefore she sought always to walk so that they who followed in her steps might not stumble."[29]

Children's Sunday School continued, with minor adjustments, into the early 2000s. While the term "Sunday School" is no longer used, programming for children is still offered on Sunday mornings. However, as with adults, the trend in children's ministry in recent years has been away from Sunday morning gatherings in favor of meeting at other times. An example is Day One Fun that began in February 1988.

Day One Fun was designed for children ages four through sixth grade. Pastors Greg and Karen Guy led that ministry as it began, and the children divided into two groups: four-year-olds to second graders and third to sixth graders. Each Sunday evening included a lesson, crafts, games, and food.[30] When it began, forty children participated, but the "new" wore off, and within a few months, participation had declined considerably, so in November 1988, the decision was made to revamp Day One Fun into a monthly program.[31] It continued in that form for several years, although by 1993, the name "Day

---

27 The Wyatt Park Christian Church *Hi-Lites*, April 19, 1936.
28 *The Call to Worship*, February 18, 1960.
29 *The Call to Worship*, February 25, 1960.
30 *The Call to Worship*, February 11, 1988.
31 *The Call to Worship*, November 3, 1988.

One Fun" was used for the youngest children, and third to sixth graders belonged to CCF, the Christian Children's Fellowship.

By 2004, children's programming had moved to Wednesday afternoons, and it had a new name, "Halos." The name meant "to encircle children with the luminous presence of God."[32] Designed for kindergarteners to sixth graders, the programming included a lesson, music, games, and crafts. Children were picked up from school, and families were encouraged to join their children after Halos for a Family Night Dinner in the Social Hall.

Five years later, it became apparent that the afternoon programming needed restructuring, with something different for the fourth to sixth graders. In terms of age, they are between younger elementary children and middle school, so THAT Club was formed. THAT stands for "Tween Here and There," and the program uses materials designed for that age group.[33] Halos and THAT Club continue, although the Wednesday programming moved to evenings in 2013.

Ministry to children is a continual work in progress, and Sunday morning programming is illustrative of that. After much discussion, prayer, and a detailed congregational survey, the decision was made in 2009 to change the Sunday morning schedule, dividing it into two blocks of time. Two worship services are conducted, with Christian education being offered concurrent with those worship services. In other words, since 2009, there has not been a *separate* time for Christian education. Overall, the schedule works well, but details of it continue to evolve, especially with ministry to children. Different options have been tried since 2009. Currently (in 2017), children are in the sanctuary for the first part of each worship service. Then they go to Children's Time, which offers a lesson tied to the worship message and does so in ways that are appropriate for children of different ages. As with other aspects of church life, ministry to children at Wyatt Park continues to adapt itself to changing circumstances and preferences.

---

32 *The Call to Worship*, December 8, 2004.

33 Board minutes, September 21, 2009.

Especially popular with children is Vacation Bible School, and it, too, has evolved. Early on, it was known as Vacation Church School. VCS looked more like a "school," was held during the day, and often lasted for two weeks. These days, VBS is held in the evening, lasts for one week, and doesn't look like a school at all. Instead, it has a festival atmosphere with boisterous, contemporary songs, elaborately decorated small group learning areas, games, crafts, and of course, food.

Exactly when Vacation Church School began at Wyatt Park is unclear, but it was first mentioned in available documents in 1943. Two worship bulletins from that time offer brief descriptions and indications that the atmosphere was definitely one of "school." VCS lasted for two weeks, began each morning at 9:00 and ended at 11:30 a.m. Mrs. Harold Olmstead served as "Dean" and there were twenty-three "faculty members." Ninety-six children participated that year.[34]

Since then, Vacation Church (Bible) School has been an annual event, with just a few exceptions. There was no VCS in 1950 due to construction of the Education Building. VCS was cancelled in 1979 because there were not enough volunteers to help, and it was cancelled again in 1983, but the reason is unclear.[35] Along the way, the popular event came to be known as Vacation Bible School (VBS), and by the early 1990s, it had made the transition to evenings and a more festival-like atmosphere. In 2010, Wyatt Park added an element to VBS that has since been picked up by other churches in the region. Older children, fourth to sixth graders, participate in a Junior Mission Trip as they serve in Jesus's name throughout St. Joseph (see chapter 6).

Vacation Bible School blesses the children of Wyatt Park certainly, but it can also be an effective way to reach children who are not connected with the church and/or are not familiar with Jesus. Fliers are distributed throughout the neighborhoods around Wyatt Park each year, and at times, VBS has been reconfigured to focus on reaching out beyond the congregation. In 1975, there was a special Vacation Church School for Exceptional Children. It was

---

34 Worship bulletins, May 30, 1943, and June 6, 1943.
35 *The Call to Worship*, June 1, 1950, May 24, 1979, and May 9, 1983.

intended for children with special needs and had as its goal "to provide opportunities for the children to experience achievement and self-identity through which they may accept themselves as persons of value and worth to themselves, to others, and to God." Barbara Crumley and Dorothy Duncan were

the organizers.[36] In 2013 and again in 2015, VBS was taken outside the church building and instead held each evening in city parks, with the goal of reaching children living in those neighborhoods.[37] In addition, since 2015, a special version of VBS has been taken to children housed at the downtown YWCA shelter for

abused women and children. Regardless of the name or location, the goal of VBS remains the same each year, to love children and to love them into a relationship with Jesus.

Ministry to Youth

For people engaged in most any type of ministry, either paid or volunteer, the work provides a mixture of joys and frustrations, good news and bad news. Rev. Lawrence Bash wrote a lengthy newsletter article in 1947, excitedly sharing many successes of the congregation's ministry to youth. While overwhelmingly positive, he did point out two examples of good news and bad news:

> Did you notice that 102 were in the two youth departments Sunday morning? (As a matter of fact, there were 108, but six boys got restless and did not remain in their class, so they were not counted).[38]

---

36 *The Call to Worship*, July 24, 1975.

37 VBS at Bartlett Park, 2013.

38 *The Call to Worship*, October 23, 1947.

In that same column, he commended the fifty Youth Choir singers who participated in worship every Sunday morning, "except for a tendency to whisper a bit. I must speak to them about that!" Joys and frustrations, good news and bad. Given Rev. Bash's consistent success with ministry to young people, it is reasonable to assume that his observations were made tongue in cheek. At least somewhat.

Ministry to youth also requires tremendous flexibility because teens can be insistent in their desire to take risks and try new things and at the same time be totally resistant to even the slightest change in customs or routines. Joys and frustrations.

One can only wonder what the atmosphere in the room must have been one night in 1948 when a risk was taken. On that night, the Christian Youth Fellowship (CYF) met, but it was an unusual meeting and was discussed favorably at the next board meeting. That particular youth group meeting included "25 colored young people" from St. Francis Baptist Temple. Schools were segregated in those days, so the youth who were gathered in that room did not go to school together and may not have even met before that night. African American students attended Bartlett High School at Eighteenth and Angelique. Most of Wyatt Park's youth attended Central, Benton, and Lafayette High Schools. Board members noted a few days later that the groups "behaved in a very orderly and congenial manner."[39] No other record of that meeting has been found, but given the condition of race relations in the 1940s, it would be interesting to know more about what went on and what, if anything, that gathering did to impact race relations among the youth who attended.

Sunday-School classes, in one form or another, have been offered to teen-agers throughout Wyatt Park's history, but by the mid-twentieth century, a significant portion of ministry to teens was taking place at times other than Sunday mornings. Exactly when a regular, organized youth group began is not known, but by the 1930s, Wyatt Park teens were gathering weekly for Christian Endeavor meetings. By 1947, the group's name had changed to

---

39 Board minutes, March 2, 1948.

Christian Youth Fellowship (CYF). That name is still used. By 1950, the group for junior high (middle-school) youth was known as Chi-Rho, and that name is also still in use.[40] Regular meetings, weekly in most years, have always been at the center of youth group life, but there have been other activities as well.

Annual youth retreats to the YMCA's Camp Marvin Hillyard were held in the 1940s and 1950s. Typically lasting two days and nights, the retreats often included guest teachers. One of the guests in 1945 was "Rev. Thomas Toler of Kansas City," who would become Wyatt Park's pastor four years later.[41]

Weekends in the early 1960s featured Friday-night events that went under different names: "Youth Flings," "Whing Dings," and "Teen Town." An October 1962 Youth Fling is pictured and was described this way in the newsletter:

Last Friday night, approximately 250 youth chose the wholesome environment of our church for social fun, in preference to less desirable surroundings. Many of these were Christians of various backgrounds, while others had no church affiliation. They came from all over St. Joseph and even from out of town.[42]

The writer also commended the congregation, "which dares to meet youth on their own perplexing battleground." The congregation's willingness to meet youth "on their own perplexing battleground" continues today.

---

40 *The Call to Worship*, May 4, 1950.

41 Worship bulletin, September 9, 1945. Camp Marvin Hillyard is still operated by the YMCA, a few miles southeast of St. Joseph.

42 *The Call to Worship*, October 18, 1962.

As with other areas of congregational life, youth groups reflect the times in which they live. Event names such as Youth Flings and Whing Dings worked well in the 1950s and early 1960s but probably would not attract much of a crowd today, that is, unless the event is billed as being "retro." An example of youth groups reflecting their times is found in the ways groups have been organized. In the 1950s, for example, Wyatt Park youth groups were *very* organized, and there is a reason for that.

Institutions were highly regarded in the post–World War II years, and so were the ways large institutions organized themselves. Smaller organizations, including churches, sought to follow the lead of larger institutions, so they formed governing boards, executive committees, programming committees, and flow charts. This newsletter item about newly elected CYF officers in 1951 is illustrative of those times:

> The Christian Youth Fellowship elected these new officers last Sunday evening: Ross Woodbury, president; Jo Ann McMaster, vice-president; Marsha Bush, secretary; Joyce Hargrove, editor of the Scoop; Roger Duncan, associate editor; Kyle Maxwell, Worship Chairman, Mary Lou Stover, Study Chairman; Carol Sue Asbury, Enlistment Chairman; Charlene Carr, Service Chairman; Jeanette Pope, vice chairman; Carolee Ricklefs, Recreation Chairman. The first meeting of this new Executive Committee was held last Monday evening at which time members were assigned to committees. Next Sunday night will be a short term planning session by committees, following which there will be an installation service of the new officers. A party will follow.[43]

Lengthy officer lists and flowcharts were part of congregational life in the mid-twentieth century. So were meetings—lots of them, as illustrated by this newsletter note to Chi-Rho members: "Come all of you Chi-Rho's and help us plan our next two meetings."[44] It was a group meeting to plan group meetings.

---

43 *The Call to Worship*, June 21, 1951.
44 *The Call to Worship*, October 8, 1953.

Times were different then. Youth group organization is much less structured now, and although there are still leaders, they no longer hold elective offices.

Cultural changes that bubbled to the surface in the 1960s had an impact on youth ministry. Participation in youth groups rose and fell, and organization became less formal. In addition, by the mid-1970s, the New Generation Singers (see chapter 3) had essentially *become* the youth program for many (but not all) Wyatt Park high-school youth. Groups struggled to function in the years following the departure of New-G, but they did continue. By the mid-1990s, something new emerged as a key ingredient of youth ministry at Wyatt Park and elsewhere—summer mission trips.

Christians traveling to distant locations to serve in Jesus's name is not new. It has gone on basically since the beginning of the faith; however, the custom of high-school-age groups going on annual, short-term mission trips is relatively new. At Wyatt Park, the custom began in 1996 and has continued every year since. There have been two guiding objectives: (1) Wyatt Park youth would serve people in need and do so in Jesus's name, and (2) they would work in a cultural setting different from their own. So far, they have traveled to:

1996—South Central Los Angeles, California (inner city)
1997—Walker, Kentucky (Appalachia)
1998—Oljato, Utah (Native American)
1999—Chicago, Illinois (inner city)
2000—San Antonio, Texas (Hispanic inner city)
2001—Mauldin, West Virginia (Appalachia)
2002—Memphis, Tennessee (inner city)
2003—Northwest Arkansas, Arkansas (rural poverty)
2004—Gary, Indiana (inner city)
2005—Cass Lake, Minnesota (Native American)
2006—Kincaid, West Virginia (Appalachia)
2007—Denver, Colorado (inner city)
2008—Benton Harbor, Michigan (inner city)
2009—Bayou La Batre, Alabama (Hurricane Katrina repairs)

2010—East Tennessee, Tennessee (Appalachia)
2011—Oljato, Utah (Native American)
2012—Minneapolis, Minnesota (inner city)
2013—Southeast Tennessee, Tennessee (Appalachia)
2014—Rosebud Reservation, South Dakota (Native American)
2015—Moore, Oklahoma (tornado recovery)
2016—Northwest Arkansas, Arkansas (rural poverty)
2017—Dallas, Texas (inner city)

I had the privilege of leading some of those trips in the late 1990s and early 2000s. The work is meaningful and significant, but the spiritual growth that participants generally experience may have the greatest impact. It comes as participants work side by side, join in evening group discussions reflecting on the day, and engage in one-on-one discussions late into the night. Mission trips involve much more than particular tasks at a mission site. They offer countless opportunities for deep connections with other believers and, most of all, with God.

CAMPS AND CONFERENCES

For most church youth, outdoor ministry provides meaningful, lasting experiences. Occasional group ski trips and float trips are long remembered, but the key word is "occasional." By contrast, camp and conference events occur annually and have been taking place for decades. Many Wyatt Park youth have grown up with summer camp as part of their yearly routine. Since 1929, youth from Wyatt Park have joined with their peers from other Christian Churches in northwest Missouri.

NOWEMO (short for northwest Missouri) began in 1929 as a "summer training school for the youth of the church." Over the twenty-plus years of its existence, NOWEMO Conferences were held at a variety of locations, including state parks, YMCA Camp Marvin Hillyard, and Tarkio College.[45] Exactly when the NOWEMO Conferences ended is unclear, but by the early 1950s,

---

45 *Yearbook*, Wyatt Park Christian Church, 1940.

attention had shifted to CYF and Chi-Rho Camps. Wyatt Park children and youth have participated in the annual summer camps every year since.[46]

For many years, the summer camps took place at different locations. Most were held in northwest Missouri, but at least two camp facilities in northeast Kansas were also used. By 1980, Christian church camps had made their home at Crowder State Park outside Trenton, Missouri, and it remains their home today.[47] Camps are held each summer for children as young as kindergarten, up through high school. As it has done for many years, Wyatt Park annually sends many campers and camp staff to spend several days outdoors, in the sanctuary that God built.

Statewide conferences took many forms and were generally geared toward high-school youth. In the 1950s, state youth conferences were often held at college campuses and sometimes included as many as one thousand youth. In the latter years of the twentieth century, Wyatt Park youth often attended the annual CRY (Christian Regional Youth) Festival, again usually held on college campuses. As times have changed and the denomination has declined, the role of statewide conferences for youth has diminished and is essentially nonexistent today.

A different type of conference took place in 1971, offered jointly by the Christian Church in Missouri and the Illinois Disciples of Christ. Thirty youth from each state were selected to participate in an International Affairs Seminar, focusing on the challenges to peace around the world. The Missouri group included two youth from Wyatt Park, Connie Miller and Michelle Keely. During the week, they spent time at the United Nations in New York

---

46 Chi-Rho Camp, 1962. Adults pictured: Bill and Marie Smith.
47 *The Call to Worship*, February 21, 1980.

and then Washington, DC, listening to multiple speakers in both locations.[48] Ministry to youth occurs close to home and in distant locales, but the goal is always the same: help youth develop a relationship with Jesus Christ, grow in their walks with him, and then be prepared to share his love wherever life may take them.

PARENTS' DAY OUT AND PRE-SCHOOL

In 1981, a new ministry to children and young families was born. It began as a Parents' Day Out that was offered one day per week. Reasoning behind the new program was briefly stated in the newsletter: "The expectation is that if parents can be afforded some time of their own, confident that their children are well cared for, they will be better parents." PDO's first day was September 15, 1981, and it initially accommodated up to thirty children.[49] Chris Danford was the first PDO Director.[50] The program grew, and by 1983 it was offered two days per week. Growth came again in 1984 when the church board approved a proposal to begin a preschool. A separate governing board was to be developed for the PDO/Pre-School, and the church board called upon the congregation to "show our total support for the program."[51] In addition to Chris Danford, others have served as Directors: Barbara Crumley, Tammy Guinn, and Catherine Hansen. The current Director, Michelle Vandevort, began her work in 2015.[52]

Presently, the PDO/ Pre-School serves some seventy children through Parents' Day Out (Tuesday, Thursday) and Pre-School (Monday, Wednesday, Friday). The program is guided by its own governing board, but it is seen as a ministry of the church and is supported by the congregation through provision of classroom space, utilities, insurance, and so forth.

---

48 *The Call to Worship*, March 4, 1971. I was also on that trip, representing First Christian Church in Plattsburg, Missouri. I was a high-school junior.

49 *The Call to Worship*, May 21, 1981.

50 Board "Mini-Minutes," filed with the *Call to Worship*, June 14, 1982.

51 Board minutes, December 17, 1984.

52 *The Call to Worship*, April 28, 2015.

"Be Prepared"

Boy Scout Troop 21 is not quite as old as Wyatt Park Christian Church, but it is close. In May 1920, there was a special meeting of the church board to consider forming a Boy Scout Troop at the church. The proposal was approved, and the first meeting was held on October 15, 1920.[53] Troop 21 was born on that day and has continued almost continuously since then. A lack of available adult leadership forced the troop to disband briefly in 1942, but the interruption lasted only a few months.[54] Not long afterward, the church board voted to give the Boy Scouts a permanent room in the church basement.[55] Meeting rooms have changed in the years since that decision, but the Boy Scouts still have their own space in the basement. It is currently located in space below the Social Hall that was constructed in 1994.

The Boy Scouts continue a long tradition of Scout Sunday on the first Sunday of February. Flags are brought into the sanctuary as worship begins, the Pledge of Allegiance and the Scout Oath are recited, and awards are presented. More than fifty years ago, the impact of scouting was noted in the newsletter, and the words are still applicable today:

> Every week many of our boys meet for training in skills and crafts, and to learn the basic fundamentals of citizenship and group participation through the scouting program in our church. Many of the men who are now most active in the local church and in business have found help and guidance in the years past through Boy Scouts of America, and are taking part now in giving the same help to the youth of today.[56]

Scouting is not limited to boys. Girl Scout troops have also met at Wyatt Park, although those meetings have been sporadic and no such group meets at the church today.

---

53 Board minutes, May 30, 1920, and November 11, 1920.
54 Board minutes, November 1942 (exact meeting date was not indicated in the minutes).
55 Board minutes, July 1943 (exact meeting date was not indicated in the minutes).
56 *The Call to Worship*, February 6, 1964.

A Few More

School for Christian Living:

From 1946 until at least 1960, Wyatt Park Christian Church joined with other congregations in the St. Joseph Council of Churches to offer a School of Christian Living. Multiple classes were offered each year, usually at multiple churches. The 1949 class listing is illustrative:

My Christian Beliefs
The Fourth Gospel
The Church's Program in Christian Education
The Use of the Bible with Children
Understanding Ourselves
Making the Most of Life[57]

Classes typically met for four two-hour sessions, and there was no charge. Most years included sessions at Wyatt Park, as well as locations downtown, South St. Joseph, and the north side.

Spratt Lectures:

For nine years (1997–2005), Wyatt Park hosted the Leah Spratt Lectures. Funded by grants from the Leah Spratt Foundation, the lectures were intended to offer continuing education to pastors and lay leaders from throughout northwest Missouri and northeast Kansas. The one-day lectures typically included three sessions, a meal, and time for discussion. The list of instructors included, among others, nationally known authors, Tex Sample and Tom Bandy.

Soup, Sandwich, and Scripture:

For several years during the 1990s, Wyatt Park hosted "Soup, Sandwich, and Scripture." Conceived as a lunchtime Bible study, the program was intended to provide brief introductions to every book of the Bible. Different local pastors

---

57 *The Call to Worship*, January 6, 1949, and January 13, 1949.

were invited to share forty-minute overviews of each book. Teaching began at 12:10 p.m. and ended at 12:50 p.m., enabling people on a lunch break to attend. For two dollars, participants received soup, a sandwich, and Bible teaching in a relaxed atmosphere.[58]

Library:

People who are growing disciples of Jesus Christ need resources, and for several decades Wyatt Park Christian Church has made resources available through the church library. Exactly when the congregation first created a church library is unknown, but the first mention of it was in a newsletter from 1951. A new library located in the former pastor's study (presumably on the second floor) was dedicated that October.[59] The library has been in its current location near the west entrance for many years. Books and videos are cataloged so they may be located easily, but that does not just happen. It requires multiple volunteers to maintain a library of the caliber that Wyatt Park offers. Joyce Rochambeau was the longtime leader of the volunteer group that also included Alice Purvis, Mildred LaBouff, Alyce DuCoing, and Barbara Dalrymple (the current library coordinator). The library was expanded as part of a 2016 renovation and now includes a media center for children as well as the familiar repository of books and video resources.

Proverbs 22:6 makes this observation: "Train up a child in the way he should go; even when he is old he will not depart from it." Each person is given life by God, so the word "child" applies to everyone. Learning about God, Jesus, the Holy Spirit, scripture, life, and how faith and life intersect is not something that someone does for a while and then graduates. Growing as a disciple of Jesus is not something one does. Growing as a disciple of Jesus is to be the way one *lives.*

---

58 *The Call to Worship*, August 25, 1994.
59 *The Call to Worship*, October 25, 1951.

CHAPTER 5

Gathered to Gather

———

And they devoted themselves to the
apostles' teaching and fellowship,
to the breaking of bread and the prayers. (Acts 2:42)

FAMILIES GATHER TOGETHER FOR MANY reasons: special meals, holiday celebrations, marking milestones, recognizing achievements, helping a loved one
in trouble, and grieving the death of a family member, to name just a few. It's
the same with church families, and for many of the same reasons. When they
function well, congregations become loving, welcoming families, and Wyatt
Park Christian Church has been described as a "family church" for decades.
As with any family, the congregation has experienced some bumps along the
way, but Wyatt Park folk have gotten through those difficult times and moved
beyond them. When all is said and done, at its heart Wyatt Park Christian
Church is a loving, welcoming family.

How many family members are there? Determining the answer is, at best, an
inexact science. Are people participating or nonparticipating members? How is
"participating" defined? What about those who actively participate over a period
of years but never formally join the church? The membership number may well
have been most exact in the congregation's early years. For example, in 1913,
the church board approved $3.06 to pay the annual assessment to the Church

Federation at a rate of $.01 per member.[1] That payment amount would indicate membership of 306 people, but there is no indication of how "membership" was defined in those days. Interestingly, total membership is rarely noted in available documents, and the membership number for many years is simply unknown. Worship attendance, Christian education participation, and financial support have been regularly published but not total membership. Based on documents that are available, Wyatt Park's membership peaked at "approximately 1300" in 1957.[2] How that number was determined is unknown. Currently (in 2017), participating membership is 643. A "participating" member is someone who has joined the church and regularly engages in congregational life.

The number of members may not have been noted very often, but church membership has been consistently presented as something of significance. Consider these excerpts from a 1953 newsletter article encouraging regular visitors to become members:

> We rejoice that there are many, many people who attend our services regularly and participate in the life and work of our church but who do not formally belong to the Wyatt Park Christian Church. At this time we would like to issue a special invitation to you to become full members. There are two good reasons why you should.
>
> First, for your own sake. The church will mean more to you when you actually belong to it. You will be establishing yourself in the life of the community in a way that is possible in no other manner. For your own sake, belong to the church.
>
> Second, for the church's sake and the world's sake you ought to belong to a church near where you live and be actively engaged in its work. The Christian life is like a railroad ticket which says, "No good if detached." In a day when the world needs Christianity so desperately—the church needs you to add to its strength and to its influence.[3]

---

1 Board minutes, June 2, 1913.
2 *The Call to Worship*, January 2, 1957.
3 *The Call to Worship*, March 12, 1953.

Regardless of the number of people who have been part of the congregation's life, sometimes it becomes necessary for family members to help one another stay in line. This note from a 1948 church board meeting is illustrative: "It was moved and carried that Board members refrain from smoking in the church and try to influence others to do likewise."[4] Almost exactly one year later, the board approved a proposal to allow smoking in the church during social gatherings but not at formal meetings.[5] It has been many years since smoking was allowed inside the building, and now smoking is prohibited anywhere on church property.

Helping one another stay in line, encouraging one another, laughing together, crying together, serving together, building together, learning together, worshiping together—an active congregation is engaged *together* in so many ways. Thankfully, much of that activity at Wyatt Park has been recorded and those records have been kept. There are board minutes, newsletters, numerous file folders, and scrapbooks. According to a 2005 newsletter article, the scrapbooks were a few years in the making:

> About three years ago, Deedie Killgore spearheaded a group who sorted through boxes of photos to start these (WPCC History) scrapbooks. That group included Vicki Gentzell, Susie Vance, Connie Heard, Minnie Lou Ray, Ellen Farmer, Ethel Thom, Marcia McKee, and Mae Bermond. In recent weeks, the scrapbooks have been completed by B. Marie Smith, Hazelene Nave, Marjorie Viestenz, and Minnie Lou Ray. Thanks to all who helped in any way. They will bring back memories for years to come.[6]

Volunteers have continued that work, maintaining scrapbooks for the years since 2005. The scrapbooks are stored in a first-floor classroom and are put out for display periodically.

---

4 Board minutes, February 3, 1948.
5 Board minutes, February 8, 1949.
6 *The Call to Worship*, April 27, 2005.

FEED THEM AND THEY WILL COME

Certain phrases have a way of immediately triggering happy memories. "Church potluck" is one of those phrases for many who have spent much time in a local church. For many older church members, and especially those who grew up in rural areas, the phrase "Dinner on the grounds" can elicit the same response. Next to worship, food has probably drawn Christians together more consistently than anything else. There is just something special about mealtime. Jesus understood that, which is why the gospels include so many stories of Jesus sharing meals, often with "tax collectors and sinners," the kinds of people others preferred to avoid. Barriers come down and tension has a way of easing when meals are shared. Gatherings around a meal tend to diminish differences and instead offer a reminder of how much people have in common.

Homebuilders Children
Picnic at Bartlett Park
1923

Church dinners have been a part of congregational life at Wyatt Park Christian Church from the beginning. One of the earliest photos is of children attending a Homebuilders Sunday School Class picnic at Bartlett Park in 1923. Dinners have been held as part of special celebrations, such as when the congregation celebrated its fifti-
eth, seventy-fifth, one-hundredth, and one hundred and twenty-fifth anniversaries. Financial campaigns have often begun and/or concluded with a meal, and dinners have accompanied the completion of construction projects. Meals have been held to welcome new pastors and to thank them for their time at Wyatt Park when their ministries come to a close. A dinner was held in 1968 to honor those who had been members of the church for at least fifty years. Twenty-six people were honored, and their membership tenure ranged from fifty years to sixty-nine years.[7] The list of reasons to have

---

7 *The Call to Worship*, November 28, 1968.

a special meal is lengthy. Of course, meals can be held for no other reason than the passage of time.

Weekly and/or monthly dinners have been a part of congregational life, off and on, for decades. A 1947 newsletter article discussed the important role of weekly dinners:

> Our Wednesday night dinners have proved a particularly valuable part of our church life. A regular weekly dinner is quite a consider-able undertaking for a church. It requires not only a strong staff for the cooking and serving of the dinners; but also a loyal congregation, interested in the work of the church to the point of consistent weekly attendance.[8]

The article goes on to note that the minister delivers a sermon during the course of the evening, with the result being that "Wednesday night becomes as much a part of church life as Sunday morning."[9] Newsletter articles in sub-sequent years indicate seasons of fluctuating attendance and meal frequency (sometimes weekly, sometimes monthly). There have been years without regular church dinners. The current (2017) practice of Wednesday Family Night Dinners began in 2004 with the advent of Halos programming for children.

Church Loyalty Month

During the mid-twentieth century, considerable attention was given to strengthening the institutional church, from local congregations to denomi-national headquarters. Beginning in 1951 and continuing for more than twenty years, Wyatt Park Christian Church observed Church Loyalty Month. It was always observed in the fall but not always during the same month. In 1954, the program was extended to six weeks in October and November. A lengthy newsletter article focused on the results of a rather detailed analysis of

---

8 *The Call to Worship*, February 6, 1947.
9 Ibid.

the congregation's 1,184 members. It noted the number of people involved in leadership or service, who worshiped regularly or just occasionally, who participated in church functions outside of worship, who were shut in, and who were totally inactive. The intention was "to strengthen our active members in their service to the church and to reach those who are only partially active or totally inactive." On the appointed Sunday, nearly two hundred callers shared a meal at the church and then called upon every member of the church. Members were encouraged to stay at home that afternoon "until the callers get to their homes."[10]

Church Loyalty Month was observed annually for more than twenty years, but activities associated with it peaked during the 1950s. The last mention of Church Loyalty Month in the newsletter was in 1973. Rev. Bill Mallotte noted it in his pastor's column, but there was no indication of any special activities.[11]

THE JOY OF FELLOWSHIP

Sometimes people need to get together for no other reason than to have some fun. That includes Christ followers, because if people who have life and hope in Jesus can't find joy, then who can? Visitors often remark that they hear a lot of laughter at Wyatt Park. That has been true for a long time. Consider an item from a "Turning Back the Pages" feature in the *St. Joseph News-Press*. It looked back forty years, to September 1927, and noted as follows: "Plans were announced for a concert, featuring only kitchen utensils, at Wyatt Park Christian Church, 27th and Olive Streets."[12] Sadly, imagination is necessary because no other details are available.

Beginning in 1959 and continuing until at least 1971, Wyatt Park offered a Family Camp at Crowder State Park near Trenton, which was held each year during Labor Day weekend. A description of the 1965 camp is illustrative:

---

10 *The Call to Worship*, October 7, 1954.
11 *The Call to Worship*, August 30, 1973.
12 *St. Joseph News-Press*, September 26, 1927.

The program will include study discussion groups, family devotions, vespers, swimming, and recreation. A feature of the camp is the "free" afternoon schedule which permits families to make their own plans.[13]

Family camps eventually came to an end, but another outdoor tradition continued off and on for many more years. All Church Picnics were held at different locations, including Big Lake State Park, Wallace State Park, and Camp Marvin Hillyard. Of course, not all seasons of the year are conducive to outdoor activities.

St. Joseph enjoys four very distinct weather seasons and occasionally experiences multiple seasons in a single day. When winter weather becomes especially harsh, just getting to the church can become a challenge, which makes for great storytelling months later when folks look back on the wintry days. On at least two occasions, the congregation formally recognized those who willingly braved harsh winter weather in order to attend worship and/or Sunday School. In 1959, they were recognized as members of the Snow and Ice Brigade, and then in 1993, they were presented "Pioneers of the Snow" certificates.[14]

When the weather is cold and people don't get out as much, "cabin fever" often develops. Wyatt Park Christian Church offered an antidote to cabin fever for several years beginning in 1990. Cabin Fever College was offered each year, typically for a few weeks in February. Each evening began with a meal, which was then followed by classes on everything from Bible studies to church history to arts and crafts, quilting, woodworking, gardening, cooking, computers, the basics of fly-fishing, and many others. A 1992 newspaper article noted that "Cabin Fever College definitely is not your typical hallowed hall of academia. There are no tests or grades here."[15] But, there was learning along with enjoyable fellowship.

---

13 *The Call to Worship*, August 12, 1965.

14 *The Call to Worship*, January 7, 1959 and "Pioneers of the Snow" certificate dated January 10, 1993, filed in scrapbook 1992–1994.

15 *St. Joseph News-Press*, February 8, 1992; *The Call to Worship*, January 25, 1990, January 31, 1991, and February 8, 1996.

In 1997 and again in 2002, dozens of Wyatt Park folk spent a week together for Joy in the Mountains. Church families vacationed together at the YMCA of the Rockies in Colorado—first at Snow Mountain Ranch and

then at Estes Park, which both border Rocky Mountain National Park. The large groups gathered for meals, but for the most part, there was no schedule so that families could enjoy time together in the Rockies.[16]

There are occasions when celebration, fellowship, and faith come together, and that sometimes happens in especially meaningful ways. Such was the case on Valentine's Day in 1997 and again in 2016 when Wyatt Park's pastors conducted wedding-vow renewal ceremonies for couples desiring to reaffirm their commitments to each other. Twelve couples renewed wedding vows in 1997, and twenty-two couples renewed their vows in 2016.[17]

Women's Groups

Women's groups have been a part of congregational life at Wyatt Park since the late 1800s, and they have consistently had a missions focus. A review of meeting minutes through the decades shows that a significant portion of each meeting has been, and still is, devoted to helping others in some way. Although their beginning dates are unknown, in the early 1900s, there were two women's groups, and both were engaged in benevolent work.

The Christian Women's Board of Missions (CWBM) organized national and global missions work on behalf of the Christian Church (Disciples of Christ), and there was an auxiliary group at Wyatt Park. As examples of their

---

16 *The Call to Worship*, January 23, 1997; Cabinet Minutes, August 19, 2002.

17 *The Call to Worship*, February 20, 1997; Board Minutes, February 16, 2016.

activities, in the summer of 1902, the Wyatt Park Auxiliary of CWBM discussed ways to help meet needs in "the Islands" (unnamed), Puerto Rico, and in the cities of Calcutta (Kolkata), India; Ann Arbor, Michigan; and Lawrence, Kansas.[18] Less than forty years after the end of the Civil War, ways to improve race relations were also occasionally discussed. Meeting minutes in 1903 include the question, "Is there a color line among the redeemed?"[19] The conclusion then was that there is no such line, a conclusion that is affirmed even more strongly today.

During that same time, the Ladies Aid Society (1910 photo) focused its attention on needs within the congregation and in St. Joseph. Both groups met jointly on occasion and at some point may have merged because by the early 1920s, there was no more mention of the CWBM Auxiliary, at least in available documents. Ladies Aid Society

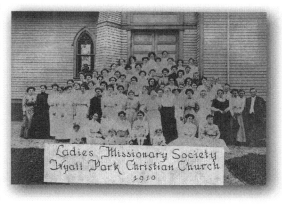

Ladies Missionary Society
Wyatt Park Christian Church
1910

meetings were monthly and typically lasted most of the day. The morning was spent in some type of activity, often sewing, followed by a noon meal. Afternoons began with worship and then continued with a business meeting. Meeting minutes give some detail about events and fund-raising efforts. Most of the money that was raised went toward local and/or global benevolent and missionary work. There were occasions when the congregation, and especially its building fund, received the proceeds from an event or activity. Funds were sometimes raised in unusual ways. For example, in March 1926, "Motion made and carried that we try to make a mile of pennies, asking our friends

18 Meeting minutes, Wyatt Park Auxiliary, Christian Women's Board of Missions, June 1902 and July 1902.

19 Meeting minutes, Wyatt Park Auxiliary, Christian Women's Board of Missions, August 1903.

to each buy a foot of pennies."[20] Subsequent meeting minutes make mention of the effort but do not indicate whether it was successful. How much money might such an undertaking raise? Probably about $845 (see note below).[21]

In 1927, the Ladies Aid Society voted to restructure itself, although the reasoning behind it is not spelled out in meeting minutes. Group members adopted the Council Plan and with that came new officers and a new name, "The Christian Women's Council."[22] Members were divided into four geographic "sections" with the dividing lines being Twenty-Seventh Street and Mitchell Avenue. From then on, part of the council's ongoing activity was conducted during general meetings, while the remainder of the work was done within the sections.[23] The 1940 yearbook provides a brief description of the council:

> The entire work of the Church, local and world-wide is supported. Educational programs are presented each month, both in meetings of the sections and at the general assembly. The Council meets the first Thursday of each month at 10:30 o'clock. The morning is devoted to the business of the organization. A covered-dish luncheon is served at the noon hour and the afternoon is devoted to the presentation of a study of missionary work.[24]

Now, more than seventy-five years later, the group still follows the same basic format when it gathers.

In 1950, the name of the group changed again, this time to "The Christian Women's Fellowship." Christian Women's Fellowship (CWF) was used across

---

20 Meeting minutes, Ladies Aid Society, March 11, 1926.

21 I was curious and determined that when laid side by side, there are 16 pennies per foot. There are, of course, 5,280 feet in a mile, leading to the following equation: $16 \times 5280 / 100 = \$844.80$. That would be a challenging but not unreasonable goal in 1926. When pennies are stacked, there are 18 pennies per inch, leading to the following equation: $18 \times 12 \times 5280 / 100 = \$11,404.80$. That total would be huge and quite unlikely as a fund-raising goal.

22 Meeting minutes, Ladies Aid Society, April 7, 1927.

23 Meeting minutes, The Christian Women's Council, May 12, 1927, and June 9, 1927.

24 *Yearbook*, Wyatt Park Christian Church, 1940.

the denomination to identify organized women's ministries.[25] As with the earlier Christian Women's Council, the total membership was divided into smaller groups, known as "Circles" instead of "Sections." There were seven Circles in 1950, and by 1956, the number had increased to thirteen. By 1959, three of the Circles met at night, a move necessitated by the cultural trend of women increasingly having jobs outside the home.[26] Cultural trends affecting worship attendance and church membership have also had an impact on the CWF. For example, in 1971 the number of Circles stood at eight, and by 1993 there were four.[27] Today (in 2017) the group is no longer divided into smaller Circles.

The CWF at Wyatt Park continues to meet on the first Thursday of each month, and the meeting format is unchanged. The group is small in number, but the benevolent work it continues to do is considerable. Multiple projects are undertaken each year, and the annual listing of those efforts easily fills two typewritten pages, single spaced. It would be impossible to know how many thousands of people have benefited from the work of Wyatt Park women's groups through the decades. Year after year, decade after decade, they have faithfully gathered, lovingly served, and generously shared—all in the name of Jesus Christ. Administrative Pastor Cindy Crouse reflected on the CWF's continuing accomplishments after attending one of the group's meetings in 2015:

> My respect for them has deepened. I listened to their reports about their many projects and I cannot help but feel very appreciative of their years of service. These women not only helped lay the foundation for their families, but they did so for our church as well. I cannot even begin to imagine the many hours they have spent serving others, teaching Sunday School classes, preparing meals, reading their Bibles, working with children in VBS, feeding the poor, and many

---

25 *Yearbook—Directory*, Wyatt Park Christian Church, 1950–1951. Today (in 2017), the denomination uses the term "Disciples Women's Ministries," but in most congregations, the name "Christian Women's Fellowship" continues to be used.

26 *The Call to Worship*, November 12, 1959.

27 *The Call to Worship*, January 21, 1971, and July 15, 1993.

other ministries too numerous to list. Our church is strong because of leaders like these ladies. Your attendance, your devotion, and your generosity bless us.[28]

Men's Groups

Men's groups started a few decades after women's groups were organized. The men met less often and for several extended periods did not meet at all. When men's groups did meet, much of their time was focused on service in the church and growing in faith. Of course, there was also time for play, as illustrated by this note from board minutes in 1942: "It was moved and carried that the Men's Club be allowed to play games, except card games, in the Social Hall."[29] When the weather allowed for it, games moved outside and to one place in particular. In fact, the men's group "playground" became somewhat of a landmark in the Wyatt Park neighborhood in the 1940s and 1950s.

Twenty-first-century summer schedules can be just as full as schedules at any other time of the year, but that was not always the case. In years gone by, summer evenings tended to be more relaxed, with neighbors visiting on front porches, couples on leisurely strolls, and friends and neighbors gathered for backyard games, sometimes followed by watermelon or ice cream. Beginning in 1942, people gathered at Twenty-Seventh and Mitchell for summer evenings playing croquet.

All Church Croquet Game
9-6-1942

The Men's Club began work on a croquet court in May 1942 near where the sanctuary is located today. After several weeks of labor, the hard surface court was ready for use,

---

28 *The Call to Worship*, March 10, 2015.
29 Board minutes, April 1942 (no specific day is indicated).

complete with lighting that made night play possible.[30] Once the court was completed, Pastor Joseph Houston suggested the club rename itself to "The Campbellite Croquet Club." While there is no evidence that name stuck, the croquet court became a popular spot on summer evenings for the next several years.[31]

Men's Club meetings were held on Wednesday evenings, so that was when crowds were biggest, but the court was in use most evenings during the summer months. And while most evenings it was just men playing croquet, women were invited on occasion. Such was the case on a Wednesday evening in August 1943, as described in the following Sunday's bulletin: "The Men's Club entertained their ladies at a Watermelon Feed Wednesday night. The ladies took over the croquet court and showed the men how to play the game. It was a big evening!"[32] Men's group sporting interests were not limited to croquet, of course.

At different times throughout the years, the church has sponsored softball teams, and on several of those occasions, a men's group served as the primary sponsor. Golf outings and fishing days have also been popular, often organized by a men's group. Currently, fishing days, especially for children, are organized by a relatively new men's group, the Genesis Men. Fellowship is a good reason to gather, but Wyatt Park men have often gathered for more serious activities also.

At the beginning of 1951, 111 men gathered for the initial meeting of a potential Layman's League. The term "Layman's League" was widely used in churches around the country, but it is unclear whether Wyatt Park's brief adoption of the name was part of a national organization for Christian men. Regardless of whether or not it was part of a national effort, the speaker at that organizational meeting discussed "the great possibilities men have for the advancement of the Cause of Christ through the Church."[33] Later that same year, the men's group changed its name from the Layman's League to "The

---

30 Worship bulletin, May 10, 1942.

31 Worship bulletin, June 21, 1942.

32 Worship bulletin, August 23, 1943.

33 *The Call to Worship*, January 18, 1951.

Christian Men's Fellowship."[34] Christian Men's Fellowship (CMF) has been used off and on since that time. "Off and on" also describes the frequency and consistency of men's group meetings through the years. There have been extended periods when no regular men's group meetings were held, but since the early 1980s, a men's group has met regularly at Wyatt Park.

From the early 1980s until the early 1990s, men gathered for a morning Men's Prayer Breakfast.[35] Meetings included food, Bible study, topical discussions, and of course, prayer. By the mid-1990s, the meeting time had moved to the noon hour, and for more than a decade men gathered to share lunch, encounter scripture, and pray together. The group even produced a cookbook in 2001 with a catchy, if questionable, title: *The Garlic Roadkill Cookbook*. It cost $7.50 per copy, sold quite well, and got considerable media attention.[36] Proceeds went toward missions ministries in the church. By 2007, the meeting time had returned to early mornings, and since that time a men's group has met weekly on Thursday mornings for breakfast, Bible study, and prayer.

Tableau

Successful ministries often begin with an idea from one person. In 1991, Susan Alderson had an idea for a drive-through living nativity two weeks before Christmas. In a newsletter article proposing her idea, she wrote:

> Scenes might be of shepherds in a field (with live sheep?); Joseph and Mary traveling to Bethlehem; angels announcing the Good News; Mary, Joseph, and the baby at the manger; the Wise Men seeking the Christ Child; carolers singing the songs of the season and trees with lighted decorations in our courtyard. I get goosebumps just thinking about the possibilities![37]

---

34 Board minutes, May 14, 1951.
35 *WPCC Program*, 1983.
36 *The Call to Worship*, January 24, 2001.
37 *The Call to Worship*, October 3, 1991.

It was an idea whose time had come and within two weeks it had a name, "Christmas Tableau."

The word "tableau" means "a depiction of a scene usually presented on a stage by silent and motionless costumed participants."[38] Wyatt Park's first Christmas Tableau was presented on December 20–21, 1991, with three scenes: a nativity, a choir singing Christmas carols, and a contemporary family at Christmas. That first year, more than four hundred cars drove through, many having waited in traffic that was backed up for three blocks.[39]

In December 1992, the *St. Joseph News-Press* did a story about that year's upcoming presentation of Tableau and noted that "Hundreds of people viewed the display in 1991, causing a modest Mitchell Avenue traffic jam on several occasions."[40] The Christmas Tableau continues to be a major, and much-loved, annual tradition a Wyatt Park.[41] In the quarter-century since Tableau's beginning, new scenes have been added and others have been updated, but the intention remains the same. In another 1992 *News-Press* article, Tableau Coordinator Susan Alderson said the purpose was to "depict the real meaning of Christmas."[42] That is still the purpose today.

---

38 https://www.merriam-webster.com/dictionary/tableau. Accessed March 29, 2017.

39 *The Call to Worship*, December 26, 1991.

40 *St. Joseph News-Press*, exact date not available. Article in 1992–1994 historical scrapbook.

41 The stable scene during Tableau, 2016. Pictured are Leslie and Charles Stone as Mary and Joseph, and Madelyn Sidwell as the angel.

42 *St. Joseph News-Press*, December 12, 1992.

"Well Done, Good and Faithful Servant"

Those words, "Well done, good and faithful servant," are included in a parable Jesus told, often referred to as "The Parable of the Talents" (Matt. 25:14–30). They are words that all Christ followers hope to hear from the Master. It would be impossible to count the number of "faithful servants" who have contributed to the life of Wyatt Park Christian Church since its beginning in 1888. For many, their names and/or details of how they served are known only to God, which, in the end, is what matters most. Still, there are some men and women whose names appear repeatedly in the congregation's history and about whom some details of their lives may be found in the available documents. Brief profiles of a few of those are presented below. This is not an exhaustive list but rather is intended to be illustrative of the faithful servants who have played significant roles in the congregation's history, who are now at home with the Lord, and whose examples can inspire all who come after them.

Dr. O. G. Weed died in October 1950, after many years of membership and service at Wyatt Park. He was an elder and a trustee, and he played a significant role in securing financing for the congregation when it moved to Twenty-Seventh and Mitchell in 1928 (see chapter 2). He also served as Sunday-School Superintendent and was a Sunday-School teacher for many years.[43]

One month after Dr. Weed's death, the congregation gathered to remember the life of *Josephine Tolin*. She was the last remaining charter member of Wyatt Park Christian Church when she died in November 1950.[44] A Kentucky native, she lived in St. Joseph for sixty-nine years and was a member of Wyatt Park for sixty-two years. As noted in chapter 1, thirty-two charter members formed the Wyatt Park congregation in the summer of 1888.

A name that appears early and often in the congregation's historical documents is *Henry L. (H. L.) Dannen*. The local businessman served as an elder and a Sunday-School teacher, and he held a variety of leadership roles. He served on the committee that oversaw construction of the new sanctuary at

---

43 *The Call to Worship*, October 26, 1950.

44 Photos and a short article, possibly from a worship bulletin, are included in the 1949–1959 historical scrapbook, p. 6.

Twenty-Seventh and Mitchell in 1928. In 1950, he served on a similar committee as it oversaw construction of the three-story education addition. He died in April 1953.[45]

Leland Becraft came to St. Joseph in 1947 to serve as director of the Community Chest, known today as The United Way. He taught the Home Builders Class for many years and became a licensed minister of the Christian Church (Disciples of Christ). He provided pulpit supply for area congregations and served as pastor of the church at Union Star for several years. He died in April 1971.[46]

Thad Danford joined Wyatt Park in December 1952, a few months after he married lifelong church member Jeannetta Sawyer. While he served the congregation in multiple ways, he is best known for something that bears his name, Danford Hall. He devoted several years to the planning, funding, and construction of the senior housing facility. Ground was broken in May 1989, but sadly, he died of a heart attack just over one month later.[47] At a mid-July 1989 meeting, the WPC Housing Board voted to name the facility "Danford Hall," noting that "Without his perseverance the project might well have never happened."[48] Residents began moving into Danford Hall in February 1990.

On consecutive days in January 1993, Wyatt Park Christian Church lost two of its longtime servant leaders. *Frank Ross* died on January 5 after a lengthy illness. He joined Wyatt Park in 1959 and actively served in one way or another for more than three decades. He served on the Property Committee and directed Saturday cleanup crews. He was an elder, and he served on multiple Steering and Search Committees. He may have been best remembered as chairman of the ushers. Longtime members recall his welcoming spirit toward all who came to worship and the way he trained other ushers to exhibit that same spirit.[49]

---

45 *The Call to Worship*, April 16, 1953.
46 *The Call to Worship*, April 22, 1971.
47 *St. Joseph Telegraph*, March 1, 1990.
48 *The Call to Worship*, July 20, 1989.
49 *St. Joseph News-Press*, January 6, 1993. Funeral Service Bulletin, Wyatt Park Christian Church, January 7, 1993.

On January 6, one day after the death of Frank Ross, *Ralph Sawyer* went home to the Lord. He was a member of Wyatt Park Christian Church for sixty-three years, and even an abbreviated list of his different places of service is impressive:

He had been Chairman of the Board longer than any other person, over twenty years through the 1940s and 1950s during the ministries of Lawrence Bash and Tom Toler. These were the growth years of Wyatt Park Christian Church. After his retirement in 1972, he became both Minister of Pastoral Care at Wyatt Park Christian Church and Pastor of the rural Bethany Christian Church near Stewartsville.[50]

He also taught several Sunday-School classes and organized a Monday night Bible study (see also chapter 8).

Laura Ream was elected elder in 1979, as was Barbara Crumley, and they became the first women to serve as elders at Wyatt Park. Elders are to be spiritual leaders of the congregation, and until 1979, the role of elder was reserved for men only. In addition to serving as elder, she was a lifelong member of Wyatt Park, taught Sunday School, and chaired numerous committees. Her service extended beyond the local church to the community, especially the YWCA, which honored her with the Outstanding Woman Leader Award. And she served on area and regional boards of the Christian Church. She died in March 1994.[51]

For thirty years, worshippers at Wyatt Park were greeted by *Curt Boyer*. With a smile and warm handshake, he ushered people into the sanctuary for worship. He served in other ways as well, especially tending to details surrounding preparation of the sanctuary for worship. He counted worship attendance each week, and in a 1999 profile, in the *St. Joseph News-Press*, he observed, "I counted the children in the nursery and now I'm counting their children in the same nursery."[52] His woodworking skills blessed the

50 *The Call to Worship*, January 14, 1993.
51 *The Call to Worship*, March 24, 1994.
52 *St. Joseph News-Press*, February 1999 (exact date unavailable).

congregation also, including the wooden cross upon which Easter lilies were displayed for many years. He died in November 2003.

Another name that appears early and often in the congregation's historical documents is *Herb Woodbury*. Through several decades of active church membership, he served as deacon, elder, and at least two terms as chairman of the board. He was a successful businessman and he served beyond the church doors. The list of civic activities that he was either involved with or led is extensive.[53] He died in 2004.

Dr. Larry Jones also died in 2004, following a lengthy battle with cancer. A lifelong member of Wyatt Park, the list of ways he served the church, the community, and his profession (dentistry) would fill many pages. Former Senior Pastor Gene Mockabee noted in the newsletter at the time of Dr. Jones's death:

> He had such an impact on all of us with his encouragement, his humor, his love, and his humble servant attitude. Dr. Larry led the way with others here and in the community to make good things happen for all. We treasure the stories of his willingness to get out in front and take risks that would open the way for all of us to benefit. The stories of front-end loaders will long be part of the folk-lore of Wyatt Park Christian Church.[54]

He also served in Jesus's name among the poor during mission trips to Jamaica and India.[55]

At the beginning of 2005, longtime member *Dwight Dannen* (son of H. L. Dannen, described above) went home to the Lord. His list of accomplishments as a businessman is long and impressive, and he brought that business and leadership expertise to Wyatt Park in multiple ways. He served on the board for many years and chaired several committees, including the Building Committee for the new sanctuary in 1957. He also worked on behalf of

---

53 *St. Joseph News-Press*, March 25, 2004, and June 17, 2014.

54 *The Call to Worship*, June 2, 2004.

55 I was blessed to serve with him during a trip to Puttur, India, in January 2000.

charitable organizations in St. Joseph, and his family provided leadership and financial support to the YMCA of the Rockies in Estes Park, Colorado.[56] One contributor to his success was a lifelong desire to learn, illustrated by his regular participation in study groups at the church and extensive reading on a variety of topics.

It is sad but true that some people die much too young, and such was the case with *David Miller*. He suffered a fatal heart attack in 2007. He was only fifty but had accomplished much during his fifty years. His obituary includes a list of some of the ways he served in Jesus's name:

> He was a lifelong member of Wyatt Park Christian Church where he was a deacon, elder, Board Moderator, Sunday School teacher and camp counselor. He served as coordinator for the Christmas Tableau and was awarded the Life Service Award. David served as a volunteer for Habitat for Humanity and was president of the board of directors. He was a past member and then sponsor of New Generation Singers.[57]

David Miller was survived by his wife, Michelle, and daughters, Brianna and Ashton, and all three continue to be actively involved at Wyatt Park.

Walter Wilson died on October 3, 2010, one day before his 101st birthday. As a longtime member of Wyatt Park, he served as an elder and also on the Property Committee. Along with his wife, Orpha, he was especially involved with landscaping around the church, including what is known today as God's Garden. He was an active member of the 50-50 Class and was the group's unofficial historian.

Alice Sawyer died in 2011, just two weeks before her one-hundredth birthday. She joined Wyatt Park in the early 1930s and served in multiple ways, including deaconess (three terms) and the Christian Women's Fellowship. She is best remembered for her thirty years as a teacher in the Junior Department,

---

56 *St. Joseph News-Press*, three articles written near the time of his death in 2005. Exact dates are not available. In 2004–2005 historical scrapbook.

57 Obituary, David Alan Miller, July 8, 2007.

specifically teaching fourth, fifth, and sixth graders. Her longtime teaching partner was Mary Kay West.[58]

Alice Purvis was a fixture around the church library and in the Christian Women's Fellowship (CWF) for more than fifty years. A quiet servant, she was also recognized as a leader and in 1978 became the first woman to hold the position of board chair at Wyatt Park.[59] A stroke in 1997 forced her to reduce her service somewhat, but she continued to serve as she was able until a few months before she died in 2011. She was eighty-six.

Grace Bartlett joined Wyatt Park Christian Church in 1968, shortly after her husband, Darryle, retired from a career in the military. From that time on, she was active in organizations that serve veterans and their families. She served in multiple ways around the church and is best remembered for her many years of involvement in, and leadership of, the Christian Women's Fellowship. Sadly, but not surprisingly, she was serving at the church when she died. She was in the church kitchen preparing tea for CWF members when she collapsed, and then she died a short time later at the hospital. That was in June 2013. She was eighty years old.[60]

Angela Crumley died in September 2014. She was forty-eight, and although she accomplished much, she is remembered even more for what she overcame. Multiple health problems affected her ability to do certain things but not her determination. She helped pioneer special education in the St. Joseph School District, lived independently for several years, and held jobs at three restaurants. At Wyatt Park, she was a faithful worshipper and participant in the life of the church. She especially enjoyed working with children.[61] During the last years of her life, she was confined to a wheel chair, and her struggles worsened. Despite all of that, her faith remained strong, inspiring all who knew her.

Bill Smith joined Wyatt Park Christian Church in 1956 and became an active servant immediately. By 1964, he was elected chairman of the board.[62]

---

58 Funeral-service manuscript, January 3, 2011.
59 *The Call to Worship*, June 22, 1978.
60 Funeral-service manuscript, July 1, 2013.
61 Obituary, *St. Joseph News-Press*, September 28, 2014.
62 *The Call to Worship*, April 16, 1964.

He is remembered for his quiet manner and deep faith. He was an elder and served the congregation in countless other ways. He and his wife, Marie, worked with youth during the 1960s, and a favorite memory of his family came from his time as a Chi-Rho (middle-school) camp counselor. The boys in his cabin would not go to sleep, so at about midnight, he said, "since you're not going to sleep, we're going on a hike." They hiked for two hours, and the boys slept well from then on.[63] He died in 2015.

As noted at the beginning of this section, this listing provides only a few examples of men and women who faithfully served the cause of Christ year after year, decade after decade, and are now home with the Lord. Their lives and dedicated service can inspire those who carry on their work today. Or as the writer of the letter to the Hebrews put it:

> Since we are surrounded by so great a cloud of witnesses, let us also lay aside every weight, and sin which clings so closely, and let us run with endurance the race that is set before us, looking to Jesus, the founder and perfecter of our faith, who for the joy that was set before him endured the cross, despising the shame, and is seated at the right hand of God. (Heb. 12:1–2)

---

63 Family memory shared during his funeral, May 15, 2015.

CHAPTER 6

Gathered to Serve and Proclaim

———

And the King will answer them, "Truly, I say
to you, as you did it to one of the least
of these my brothers, you did it to me." (Matt. 25:40)

And Jesus came and said to them, "Go therefore and make
disciples of all nations, baptizing them in the name of the Father
and of the Son and of the Holy Spirit." (Matt. 28:19–20)

"MISSIONS" IS A FREQUENTLY USED, but sometimes fuzzy, word having to do with the basic purpose for the church of Jesus Christ. For some, the basic calling of Christ followers is summed up by Jesus's words in Matthew 25: "As you did it to one of the least of these my brothers, you did it to me." They believe that the top priority of Christians is to care for the "least," those who are hurting, beaten down, oppressed, on the margins, or slipping through the cracks of society. Followers of Jesus are to feed the hungry, clothe the naked, visit the sick and imprisoned, shelter the homeless, and so forth. Benevolent work.

For others, the basic calling of Christ followers is summed up by Jesus's words in Matthew 28: "Go therefore and make disciples of all nations." Christians, first and foremost, are to evangelize, proclaim the gospel, and lead people to salvation, into a saving relationship with God through Jesus Christ. Soul winning.

As with much of what Jesus taught, "missions" is not *either* benevolent work *or* soul winning, but rather both. They are two sides of the same coin, and throughout its history Wyatt Park Christian Church has been reasonably successful at keeping the two in balance. There have certainly been times when one or the other priority has prevailed, but in general the two have been held together. That was true even in the congregation's early days. Board meeting minutes from December 1918 are illustrative, showing that both benevolent and evangelistic work received support:

Foreign Missions	$65
American Missions	$65
Christian Women's Board of Missions	$30
Education	$55
Church Extension	$35
Benevolence	$35
Ministerial Relief	$55
Temperance	$10
Christian Union	$10
State Missions	$55
County and District	$30
Total	$445[1]

Evangelistic revivals were common in the early days, as were special dinners and other events to raise money for a variety of benevolent causes. A good balance was maintained for the most part, but circumstances beyond the congregation's control sometimes intruded, and in those times caring for other people moved front and center.

MISSIONS MINISTRY IN WAR TIME
World War I is the earliest military conflict mentioned in congregation documents. Board minutes from June 1917 indicate that the congregation wished

---

1 Board minutes, December 2, 1918

to do what it could to support those in combat. A motion was approved "that the Ladies Aid Society be given the basket collection of any Sunday morning excepting next Sunday morning for the purpose of helping make supplies for the Battleship Missouri."[2] That decision came just two months after the United States entered World War I, also referred to as the "Great War" or "the war to end all wars." All wars are horrible, and sadly World War I did not end all wars. Less than a quarter-century later, the United States was embroiled in World War II, which influenced the congregation in multiple ways. In fact, it touched Wyatt Park Christian Church more directly than any other armed conflict in which the United States has been involved. Later wars in Korea, Vietnam, and the Middle East were felt of course, and in each of those conflicts, members of the congregation and/or their loved ones served in the armed forces. Consequently, each military conflict resulted in anxious moments, much prayer, and relief when those serving in uniform came home safely. But, because of its duration and global scope, World War II touched Wyatt Park Christian Church more deeply than any other war.

In 1943, Roger Pope chaired a new War Services Committee. It quickly established a Service Roll enabling the congregation to keep track of those who were serving in the military.[3] Within a couple of months, church members were encouraged to write down two or three names and addresses each week and write to those serving in the armed forces. By November 1943, there were seventy-four men and women from Wyatt Park Christian Church serving in the military around the world.[4] A newsletter, *The Welcome News*, was prepared weekly and sent to all who served in the armed forces. The newsletter provided information about other men and women from the congregation serving in uniform, and it also included a bit of news from home.[5]

---

2 Board minutes, June 4, 1917.
3 Worship bulletin, June 6, 1943.
4 Worship bulletin, November 7, 1943, and November 21, 1943.
5 Worship bulletin, October 31, 1943.

Sad news was shared with the congregation in July 1944. It appeared in the July 23 worship bulletin:

We are sorry to announce the first casualty on our honor roll. Everett Hegstrom was killed D-Day. Everett was a paratrooper. The church extends sincere sympathy to Mrs. Hegstrom and family.[6]

Two weeks later, a Service of Memory was conducted as part of the morning worship service. It honored Everett Hegstrom and Lieutenant C. W. Kline Jr.[7] The Service of Memory began with a prayer that included these beautiful words of hope in the midst of war:

We believe that life is eternal; that love is immortal; that death is only a horizon; and that a horizon is nothing save the limit of our sight. Lift us up, strong Son of God, that we may see further; cleanse our eyes that we may see more clearly; draw us closer to Thyself, that we may know ourselves nearer to our beloved who are with Thee. And while Thou dost prepare a place for us, prepare us for that happy place, that where they are and Thou art, we too may be. Amen.[8]

February 1945 brought news about the son of a new church member missing in the Philippines. Lieutenant Gerald Long had been missing since early January.[9] Available documents do not indicate whether he survived or not, but it was a happy ending for another church member who was missing in action. Lieutenant Max Curtis, a B-17 pilot, was reported missing in action in Germany in April 1945, but two months later the bulletin joyfully noted that he was present in worship.[10]

---

6 Worship bulletin, July 23, 1944.

7 No other information about Lieutenant Kline is available in the congregation's documents.

8 Worship bulletin, August 6, 1944.

9 Worship bulletin, February 11, 1945.

10 Worship bulletin, April 15, 1945, and June 17, 1945.

By early summer of 1945, the war was over in Europe, and victory over Japan came in August. A long, costly, global war had come to an end, and men and women serving in the military were finally able to return home. Worship bulletins in July and August listed the names of Wyatt Park members, sons, and daughters who returned home safely. On August 19, 1945, the congregation joined to prayerfully seek God's help in dealing with the aftermath of war and with moving forward. Because of the timeless needs and desires expressed by what they prayed in unison that day, the "Litany of Dedication" is offered in its entirety here:

Leader: To the patient acceptance of all the personal burdens which this war has brought upon us; to the complete sharing of all the sacrifices borne in our common cause; to the healing of all losses and devastation;

Congregation: With God's help, we do now dedicate ourselves.

Leader: To the preservation of our dearly bought and cherished freedoms for which such sacrifices of blood have been made;

Congregation: With God's help, we do now dedicate ourselves.

Leader: To the seeking and support of all ways and plans for the cooperation of nations now estranged; and of all efforts for the establishing of a world order of justice and peace;

Congregation: With God's help, we do now dedicate ourselves.

Leader: To every struggle for justice both at home and abroad; to every effort seeking to ensure all men their native right to fullness of life;

Congregation: With God's help, we do now dedicate ourselves.

Leader: To the continuance and creation of homes, rich in love and tenderness, and of a community which shall make every homecoming a glad anticipation;

Congregation: With God's help, we do now dedicate ourselves.

Leader: To such self-discipline of our minds through thought and study; to such preparation of our hearts through confession and prayer, that we may take part in realizing a world of justice and enduring peace;

Congregation: With God's help, we do now dedicate ourselves.

Leader and Congregation: O Lord, hear these our high resolves; and by the guidance of thy spirit and the continuance of thy watchful care, help is to be true to these commitments which we have now made on this solemn occasion.[11]

Sadly, prayers for justice and peace are needed today, just as much as they were at the end of World War II.

Dealing with the aftermath of war continued throughout 1945 and beyond. In November, a plea was made for extra financial contributions to help people in Europe recover from the destruction and get through the coming winter while living in difficult conditions. A minimum goal of $1,000 was set for European relief, and by mid-January, Wyatt Park members had raised $1,521. The funds were sent to Europe through the World Council of Churches.[12] Just as the need for prayer continues, so does the need to provide relief to war victims. Christians join with other people of goodwill in looking forward to the day when prayers for peace and relief for victims of war will no longer be needed.

GOOD NEWS FOR A HURTING WORLD

In a world with too much war, corruption, and poverty, there is a need for good news, and Christians believe they have what the world needs in the gospel (the word "gospel" means "good news") of Jesus Christ. Granted, the message of Jesus has not always been handled well by people claiming to be his followers, but surveys consistently show that Jesus himself is highly regarded, even by people of other faiths or who have no religious faith at all.

Although less frequent today, evangelistic revivals were common during the opening decades of Wyatt Park's history. Revivals typically included a guest evangelist and took place during consecutive evenings over a one-week period. That formula was repeated multiple times at Wyatt Park, although the

---

11 Worship bulletin, August 19, 1945.

12 Worship bulletin, November 25, 1945, and January 13, 1946.

congregation did host one evangelist for three weeks in late 1906. According to the *St. Joseph News-Press*, Rev. H. A. Northcutt of Knox City, Missouri, was known "as one of the most successful evangelists in the country. He is a speaker of rare eloquence and force, in no wise given to pyrotechnics." During the Wyatt Park revival, he was joined by Frank Huston of Indianapolis, "a popular singer who recently returned from Europe where he was engaged in revival work."[13] Newspaper articles described well-attended gatherings each night, although winter weather impacted attendance on at least some of the evenings. The three-week revival was considered a huge success, but sadly, for Rev. Northcutt it would be his last. He suffered a fatal heart attack a few days later while visiting the home of his daughter in Mexico, Missouri.[14]

Revivals continued to be a regular part of Wyatt Park's congregational life until the mid-twentieth century but were rare thereafter. The last revival at Wyatt Park was in February 1991, when people gathered for three evenings to worship and hear the gospel proclaimed by Atlanta pastor Cynthia Hale. In contrast to many multi-night revivals, attendance increased each night of that revival.[15]

There have been occasions when Wyatt Park Christian Church worked to help facilitate a citywide revival. For example, Wyatt Park's board supported efforts to bring world-renowned evangelist Billy Sunday to St. Joseph. On at least two different occasions, in 1915 and again in 1920, the board voted to endorse and financially support efforts to bring the famous evangelist to St. Joseph.[16] It was a lofty goal because "Until Billy Graham, no American evangelist preached to so many millions or saw as many conversions—an estimated 300,000."[17] Those efforts were apparently unsuccessful because no further mention of his potential appearances in St. Joseph has been found in available documents.

---

13 *St. Joseph News-Press*, November 17, 1906. A bound collection of newspaper articles from that time is kept with other records from Wyatt Park's early decades.

14 *St. Joseph News-Press*, December 20, 1906.

15 *The Call to Worship*, March 7, 1991.

16 Board minutes, April 15, 1915, and June 7, 1920.

17 *Christianity Today*, May 2017.

Eighty years later, Wyatt Park joined with other congregations to bring an evangelist with the Billy Graham Association to St. Joseph. For four nights in April 1999, Dr. Ralph Bell preached to large crowds at Spratt Stadium on the campus of Missouri Western State University. Wyatt Park joined with more than a dozen other churches to provide local organization for the event, named the "Heartland Celebration."[18]

As noted at the beginning of this chapter, "missions" is a two-sided coin with emphasis on both benevolent and evangelistic work. Evangelistic work also has two sides. Regular worship services and revivals illustrate one side—creating events and activities that encourage people to *come* to the church or some other gathering place to hear the gospel. There is another side—*going out* into the neighborhood and larger community to share the good news of Jesus. Visitation campaigns were a frequent part of Wyatt Park's congregational life during the middle decades of the twentieth century, as a campaign in October 1946, illustrates. The Visitation Evangelism Campaign opened on Sunday evening with a message from Rev. Clayton Potter of Springfield.[19] During the week, volunteers gathered at the church each evening. Their evenings began with a meal, and then they went out into neighborhoods throughout the city to call on people who might become new followers of Jesus and/or members of the church. Fifty-two people united with Wyatt Park during the three week-ends after the visitation campaign concluded.[20]

Visiting potential new members of the church was an ongoing effort for at least twenty years through the work of the Andrew Club. Formed in 1946, the club took its name "from the disciple of Jesus who was constantly bringing someone to the Master."[21] Meeting frequency varied, but the group's meeting format was consistent: gather for dinner and then go out to call on people who had shown some interest in the church. The Andrew Club functioned until at least 1966.[22]

---

18 *The Call to Worship*, April 28, 1999.

19 Rev. Potter became pastor at Wyatt Park Christian Church in 1959 (see chapter 8).

20 *The Call to Worship*, October 17, 1946, October 31, 1946, November 7, 1946, and November 21, 1946.

21 *The Call to Worship*, March 10, 1955.

22 *The Call to Worship*, October 6, 1966.

Church growth was significant in the post–World War II years, continuing through the 1950s. One consequence was an overused phone line, which resulted in the addition of a second line in 1958 with a new number, 232-3374, the number that is still in use today.[23] Growth continued as the 1960s began, illustrated by sixty baptisms in 1960, the most of any Christian Church in Missouri that year.[24]

In 1963, Evangelism Department chairman Charles "Bud" Salanski wrote a newsletter column in which he discussed the existing evangelism program and its need for additional volunteers to carry out the work. In bold type, and appropriately so, he summarized the point of evangelistic work in the local church:

> Evangelism is the primary task of the Church. Until our whole church has a feeling of concern for others and a real desire to lead them to Christ, we are not really doing our job. When I dare project into my children's world and their children's world, I see no hope except through the Church. So we must try.[25]

A newsletter column in 1974 listed several ways that individuals could share their faith and a series of similar articles appeared in the early 2000s. In 2012, the pastor's column in the newsletter included excerpts of an e-mail sent by a young woman in the congregation. Shared with her permission, the e-mail described her experience with stepping out in faith to share her faith:

> The opportunity arose at work while two co-workers and I were talking over lunch. I don't remember now what initially led to the topic. All I remember is one co-worker saying that she envied people with strong faith because she could see it in them. She wished she could have that. I hesitated for a minute, but I knew I had to say something.[26]

---

23 *The Call to Worship*, May 7, 1958.
24 *The Call to Worship*, February 2, 1961.
25 *The Call to Worship*, October 24, 1963.
26 *The Call to Worship*, July 24, 2012.

She went on to share that her decision to lean on God had gotten her through a very difficult situation and that her faith had made a significant difference in her life. She concluded, "I felt good about sharing, and now that I have done it once I feel confident about doing it again."[27]

MAKE DISCIPLES OF ALL NATIONS

Christians are called to share the gospel and embody the love of Jesus and to do so across the table, across the neighbor's fence, across town, across cultural and economic divides, and across the continents. In other words, followers of Jesus are called to share his love and their faith wherever they may be. Nowadays, air travel makes it much easier to go to distant lands, and that is done with some frequency. Throughout much of Wyatt Park's history, however, travel was difficult, so the congregation supported the work of others who served the cause of Christ in distant places. In the congregation's early years, much of that work was supported through the Christian Women's Board of Missions Auxiliary at Wyatt Park (see chapter 5). Since then, Wyatt Park's support of, and active participation in, global mission work has been extensive, illustrated by the examples that follow.

Paraguay:

In 1946, the congregation undertook continuing support of a missionary, Allin Sharp. The Kentucky native and his wife, Betty, were sent by the Christian Church (Disciples of Christ) to Paraguay in South America for rural mission work. He was supported by Wyatt Park as a "Living Link Missionary," the term used for denominational missionaries whose work was underwritten by a local congregation. For the next sixteen years, the church provided continuing financial support and regularly sent supplies and gifts. The Sharps visited St. Joseph on at least three occasions during those sixteen years, and they sent frequent written reports. One

---

27 Ibid.

such report was printed in two parts in *The Call to Worship* in May 1949. He described their visit to a farm owned by a man with whom they had become acquainted:

> We spent the whole day talking with him and his family and teaching the Scriptures. They were very receptive and said that they wanted to learn more and that they believed we taught the Truth. Last Sunday the father and his three children were in our Sunday School. The mother would have come but she had to stay to guard the house. Very few Paraguayan families go away from home all at one time. Somebody always stays to guard the house and stock.[28]

Allin Sharp was a Living Link missionary until 1962. His last visit to St. Joseph was in 1971, when he served as a local church pastor in Morgantown, West Virginia.[29]

China:

Serving on the mission field in distant lands can be dangerous, and such was the case for a missionary couple with whom Wyatt Park Christian Church had a relationship for more than fifteen years. Oswald and Irene Goulter worked as missionaries in China from 1922 until 1951. They served in the area around Hefei in eastern China's Anhui Province. During World War II, Irene Goulter was evacuated to the United States, but Oswald Goulter was held by the Japanese, and he remained interned until the war was over. Japanese troops overran their mission compound, and it needed extensive reconstruction after the war. Wyatt Park Christian Church assumed the $8,000 cost of rebuilding the five buildings in the compound.[30]

The Goulters were able to return to their work in China but not for long. Communist rebels under the leadership of Mao Tse-tung took control of China in 1949 and over time drove out all foreign missionaries, including

---

28 *The Call to Worship*, May 19, 1949, and May 26, 1949.

29 *The Call to Worship*, July 1, 1971.

30 *Yearbook*, Wyatt Park Christian Church, 1948.

the Goulters, who were forced to leave in 1951. After returning to the United States, Dr. Goulter became a professor of Christian Missions at Phillips University in Oklahoma.[31] They maintained contact with Wyatt Park and visited on occasion. Their last visit was in June 1963.[32]

Puerto Rico:

Once the rebuilding project in China was completed, Wyatt Park undertook a construction project in Puerto Rico. The year was 1950, and missionaries had been at work in the US territory for decades. They not only encountered considerable resistance but also made great strides turning large numbers of people to evangelical Christianity. As a result, the need for churches was great. Wyatt Park committed $3,000 to help build a simple church building in Bayamon, near the northeastern coast of Puerto Rico. Christians in Puerto Rico provided $2,000 toward the project.[33]

Africa:

Another project was undertaken in 1953 when Wyatt Park committed to provide a boiler and sterilizer (autoclave) for the hospital at a mission station in Wema, Kenya. Prior to that, no good method of sterilization was available.[34]

Fifty-five years later, Wyatt Park had its next direct connection with mission work in Africa. In 2008, two young women from the congregation, Laura Price and Sarah Danford, traveled to Zambia to work for two months with All Kids Can Learn International, a mission dedicated to serving children orphaned by the HIV/AIDS epidemic. That mission is operated by Benedict and Kathleen Schwartz, parents of Wyatt Park's Pastor to Children and Youth at the time, Jessica Schwartz Stan.[35]

---

31 *St. Joseph News-Press*, November 15, 1952.

32 *The Call to Worship*, June 6, 1963. The story of the couple's experiences on the mission field is told in the book *Scattered Seed: The Story of the Oswald Goulters, Missionaries to China*, written by Wilfred Powell. The book is available in the WPCC Library.

33 *The Call to Worship*, November 2, 1950.

34 *The Call to Worship*, January 22, 1953, and May 21, 1953.

35 Administrative cabinet minutes, January 21, 2008.

Currently, Wyatt Park's connection with Africa is through Rescued Readers, an organization cofounded by Wyatt Park member Beth Zahnd and Tammy Flowers. Both are public-school teachers, and the group began with the purpose of placing books in school libraries in rural Uganda. Although that purpose remains, the group's work has expanded in partnership with Children's HopeChest, a faith-based organization that seeks to transform the lives of vulnerable children and their communities.[36]

Jamaica:

Men and women from Wyatt Park Christian Church have served annually on the mission field in Jamaica since 1991. It began with a group of eight people from Wyatt Park joining with people from other Disciples of Christ Churches to do reconstruction work at Oberlin High School. Located in the mountains of eastern Jamaica, the school was damaged by Hurricane Hugo in 1989 and then by fire in 1990.[37] Annual mission trips to the area around Oberlin High

School continued until the early 2000s when the focus shifted west to the Black River area of southwestern Jamaica.

A partnership was formed with two congregations in the villages of Cambridge and Holland, and that partnership continues today.[38] Doctor Tom and Susan Alderson annually assemble a team of two-dozen-or-so medical and dental professionals and helpers. They work for a week conducting clinics organized by the two partner congregations. Numbers from the 2015 trip are illustrative of the annual trips:

---

36 Home page, accessed May 1, 2017, www.hopechest.org.

37 *The Call to Worship*, November 23, 1990.

38 The photo is from the 2016 mission trip to Jamaica. Dr. Tom Alderson is pictured, treating a patient.

2052 people received treatment of some type. The dentists extracted 292 teeth; the eye team provided glasses to 331 people; medical saw 1085 people; 361 lab tests were run, 63 echo cardiograms were done, 42 pap smears were done, and 4008 prescriptions were filled.[39]

Returning to the same location each year allows bonds to form, and deep relationships have developed between the Jamaica Mission Team and people in those two Jamaican communities. The pastor at the two churches, Gerald Emmanuel, has visited Wyatt Park, leading to a relationship between the congregations. Such relationships are not limited to Jamaica.

India:

Relationships begin in various, and sometimes roundabout, ways, and such is the case with the relationship between Wyatt Park and the Good Shepherd Mission in Puttur, India. Henry and Viola Bhasker, both educators, began caring for a few children in the 1970s, and their work grew into a mission that today includes orphanages, a hospital, dental clinic, HIV/AIDS clinic, housing for elderly, and more than a dozen village churches. In 1991, a Methodist congregation in Mohnton, Pennsylvania, began a partnership with the Bhaskers, and in 1996, the Mausolf family moved from that community and congregation to St. Joseph and Wyatt Park. The door was opened to a relationship between Wyatt Park and Good Shepherd.

Jeanette Mausolf and I traveled to India with a group from the Pennsylvania congregation in 1998, and additional Wyatt Park members joined a similar trip in 2000. From that point on, Wyatt Park trips were organized separately from the Pennsylvania congregation. Trips to India have occurred every three to five years and typically include a combination of benevolent work and evangelism. Monthly financial support of the Good Shepherd Mission began in March 2000 and continues today.[40]

39 *The Call to Worship*, February 24, 2015.
40 Administrative cabinet minutes, March 2, 2000.

Henry and Viola Bhasker visited Wyatt Park in 2001, and they were in St. Joseph at the time of the September 11 terrorist attacks. It was a frightening, emotional time, and their travel plans were complicated due to airport closures in the days following the attacks. Sadly, Viola died two years later, but Henry has continued to visit St. Joseph, as has his son, Praveen, who has a growing leadership role at the mission.

As the twenty-first century began, Wyatt Park was present in two additional locations in India. Three years after graduating from the University of Missouri, Anne Walters began work in southwestern India with Freedom Firm, a ministry that works to rescue young girls who have been sold into the sex trade.[41] During her nearly three years in India, she used horses as a way to connect with, and restore hope to, girls whose lives and spirits had been broken by sex traffickers.[42] Her ministry there concluded in 2011, the same year that Erin Raffensperger's work in India began. After graduating from the University of Minnesota in May 2011, she left for Calcutta, India, to work for a year with International Justice Mission. That Christian organization works on social justice issues around the world. In Calcutta, the group focuses on rescuing young women sold into the sex trade. Hers was a one-year internship, and when it concluded, she returned to the United States.

The Philippines:
Many people feel called to short-term mission trips to distant lands, but once in a while, the calling evolves from short-term trips into a permanent move to the foreign mission field. Such was the case for Annetta Heckman. After more than a dozen short-term trips to the Philippine island of Mindanao, she surrendered to the call to full-time mission work with Fruitful Harvest International Ministry in 2015.[43] She works at the organization's mission compound near Surigao City. Wyatt Park members send monthly financial support, and in 2016, the congregation took on a project to raise funds for

---

41 Board minutes, April 21, 2008.
42 *The Call to Worship*, April 5, 2011.
43 *The Call to Worship*, January 20, 15.

construction of a girls' dormitory, which was completed in early 2017. In addition to providing housing for female Bible students, the structure also includes permanent housing for Annetta.

CHILDREN IN MISSIONS

The calling to serve other people in Jesus's name and to share the good news of the gospel is not limited to adults. Children are also encouraged "to be and to share" the gospel of Jesus Christ. During much of the first half of the twentieth century, Wyatt Park joined other Christian churches around the country to observe Children's Day. Missions ministry was the focus of the day, and a special offering was taken for world missions. Children's Day began in 1880 at a church in Kansas when two small children brought their savings to their church to "give to missions."[44]

It has been many years since the last Children's Day observance, but children are very much involved in missions work—directly and locally. Since 2010, the annual Vacation Bible School program (VBS) has included a Junior Mission Trip. Fourth to sixth graders spend each evening of VBS out in the community serving in some way, always in the name of Jesus.

One of those evenings each year is spent at the downtown YWCA, specifically playing with children housed in the shelter for abused women and children. Following such a visit in 2015, a letter was received from the YWCA training coordinator and her letter included this:

> One of our moms said, "My boys were so excited to be able to hang out with quality men who didn't hit them. It made me realize how important it is for me to continue my process, leaving my situation." I hope your youth realize that they can make a difference with God's love and that your church has touched a family's life.[45]

---

44 *The Call to Worship*, May 30, 1956.
45 *The Call to Worship*, July 14, 2015.

Wyatt Park fourth to sixth graders also join with children from other churches in St. Joseph for iServe. iServe is intended to help children grow as disciples of Jesus as they spend three days in the early summer serving people in need and doing so alongside children from other churches and denominations. Wyatt Park children have participated in iServe annually since 2012.

SOMETIMES THEY COME HERE

Opportunities to serve other people sometimes involve those people coming here. Such was the case in 1962 when the Wyatt Park congregation sponsored a foreign exchange student from Germany. Christel Hezinger was sixteen years old when she arrived in St. Joseph in August 1962. During her school year in St. Joseph, she lived with Bill and Marie Smith and attended Central High School. Sunday-School classes and youth groups raised the needed funds to underwrite her participation in the exchange program.[46]

During the early and mid-1960s, refugees from Cuba were desperate to move to the United States. The Communist Party and dictator Fidel Castro were in control of the island nation, and Cuban families longed for freedom. Congregations across the United States joined in an effort to help families resettle, and Wyatt Park's Outreach Department worked with a national organization to sponsor one of those families. In April 1965, the family of Pedro Gonzalez was due to arrive in St. Joseph. Outreach Department members and other volunteers worked to prepare what would become their new home at 2612 Penn Street. Sadly, the family's four-year-old son became too ill to make the move.

A second family was identified, and by the end of April 1965, Santos Lopez, his wife, and young daughter arrived in St. Joseph, two months after leaving their home in Cuba. Their journey was difficult and expensive and resulted in most of their possessions being confiscated by the Cuban government. Interestingly, although it appears that the family was successfully

---

46 *The Call to Worship*, May 10, 1962.

resettled in St. Joseph, there is no further mention of them in either the news-letter or board minutes.[47]

IGLESIA CHRISTIANA PAN DE VIDA

In 2005, Triumph Foods opened a large pork processing facility in St. Joseph. The plant opening, along with the opening of related facilities, led to an increase in the city's Hispanic population. It also resulted in the need for Hispanic places of worship, and for just over a year, a Hispanic congregation worshiped at Wyatt Park Christian Church. Iglesia Christiana Pan De Vida held its first worship service in June 2008. David Ramirez came to St. Joseph from Texas to serve as pastor, and the congregation met each Sunday in the large, multipurpose room below the Social Hall. Within a few months, worship attendance averaged forty people.[48] Both congregations joined for a bilingual service on Christmas Eve, 2008. It was an emotional experience as all elements of the service were done in both English and Spanish.

Planting a new congregation is challenging work, and most close soon after they open. Such was the case with Iglesia Christiana Pan De Vida. As 2009 began, attendance and participation started to decline, and by mid-summer the congregation decided to close. A few weeks later, Bill Rose-Heim, Northwest Area Pastor of the Christian Church in Mid-America, wrote a letter of thanks to the Wyatt Park congregation, and his letter included this:

> Nesting a new congregation is anything but simple. Add to the mix challenges of language, cultural differences, levels of ability, and lim-ited resources and a host congregation can soon find itself giving far more than might have originally been anticipated. Wyatt Park Christian Church was an outstanding host and a true partner in every sense of the term. I cannot adequately describe the invaluable

---

47 *The Call to Worship*, March 11, 1965, March 18, 1965, April 8, 1965, April 22, 1965, and April 29, 1965.
48 Board minutes, September 15, 2008.

assistance given by the pastoral staff and members who repeatedly went out of their way to demonstrate hospitality and offer much needed support.[49]

Despite the challenges that go with "nesting" (hosting) another congregation in the building, there was sadness at Wyatt Park when the Hispanic congregation closed and widespread expressions of a willingness to do it again should the opportunity arise.

WALK OUT THE DOORS—ENTER THE MISSION FIELD

Serving in Jesus's name and proclaiming the gospel ("missions") in faraway places is important and often rewarding work. Of course, traveling to distant places is not necessary because there is also work to be done close to home. The congregation is frequently reminded that the mission field is right outside the doors, and throughout Wyatt Park's history, church members have given of themselves to serve and to share the gospel in the St. Joseph area.

Since its beginning in 1888, Wyatt Park Christian Church has provided financial support to faith-based organizations that either serve people in need or that join together to proclaim the gospel of Jesus Christ. In addition to support from the congregation itself, members are encouraged to offer financial and volunteer support to other charitable organizations in the city.

During the 1950s, the congregation instituted "The Outward Circle," a concept that was described in the newsletter:

We enter into the worship of the church that the Presence of Christ might be renewed in us. But we turn outward, that His love may be reflected through our lives into all the world. That is the "Outward Circle."[50]

---

49 *The Call to Worship*, September 1, 2009.
50 *The Call to Worship*, October 14, 1954.

At regular intervals, Wyatt Park members were invited to report on their service in the community, indicating what they did and for whom. Individual names were never disclosed, but summaries of those reports were published in the newsletter, and they consistently showed well over one hundred congregation members actively giving of themselves in the mission field located just outside the church doors.

Wyatt Park has partnered with many faith-based groups over the years, and three of those partnerships have been especially strong in recent decades. InterServ is an interdenominational social services ministry that began in

1909. From infants to senior citizens, people in need benefit from the organization's programs. Wyatt Park provides financial support, and church members volunteer in a variety of ways, usually as individual volunteers, but sometimes in a coordinated manner. For several years, Wyatt Park youth have served at InterServ's Calvin Center

Food Pantry sorting food that is donated during December food drives.[51] Another food drive known as Souper Bowl coincides with the NFL Super Bowl, and to help spur more donations, Wyatt Park Stadium was constructed in 2008 and is used annually. Church members are encouraged to fill the stadium with food.

In 1888, the same year that Wyatt Park Christian Church was formally organized, the St. Joseph YWCA opened its doors. It has served women in multiple ways since then, including a shelter for women and their children who are fleeing abusive homes. In recent years, Wyatt Park members have served shelter residents. There has been work with the children staying in

---

51 *St. Joseph News-Press*, December 22, 1996.

the shelter (see chapter 4 and also this chapter). And for several years a small group of volunteers from the church arrived at the YWCA well before dawn on Thanksgiving morning and spent several hours preparing a Thanksgiving meal for the women and children in the shelter.[52]

Wyatt Park Christian Church has, at times, partnered with Habitat for Humanity to build a home. Former Wyatt Park Senior Pastor Gene Mockabee played a key role in establishing a St. Joseph chapter of Habitat for Humanity, which makes it possible for families to own a home when they would not otherwise be able to do so through normal buying and financing channels. Through Habitat for Humanity, a family buys the home but at a reduced price. Part of their payment is "sweat equity," hours that the family spends working alongside Habitat staff and volunteers as their home is built. In 1996, Wyatt Park members helped build St. Joseph's first Habitat house, which was near Krug Park. Members of the congregation have helped build other homes, and they joined with members from other churches for two special construction projects. In 2001, members of several churches came together to construct a home on Edmond Street, dubbed "Harmony House." Ten years later, in July 2011, Wyatt Park joined with other churches for a "blitz build." The goal was to build a home in one week, and the goal was met.[53]

For most people Christmas Eve and Christmas Day are holidays but not for first responders and medical personnel. They are on duty 24-7 for 365 days, so in 2006 a tradition began at Wyatt Park that continues today. Members of the OK Class solicit donations of Christmas goodies and volunteers to help fill and deliver boxes of Christmas treats. On Christmas Eve, they deliver the treats to St. Joseph fire stations, the Law Enforcement Center, Buchanan County EMS, and the Emergency Room at Mosaic Hospital.[54] As is often the case in missions ministry, the ones delivering the boxes derive as much joy as the ones receiving them.

---

52 *The Call to Worship*, December 6, 2011.

53 *St. Joseph News-Press*, July 6, 2001, and *The Call to Worship*, July 5, 2011. Additional source: e-mail from Gene Mockabee to the author dated May 12, 2017.

54 *The Call to Worship*, January 4, 2007.

Jacobs Closet is another ministry that originates inside the church building, but it exists to serve people throughout St. Joseph. Specifically, Jacob's Closet provides clothing, free of charge, to children in need. Since February 1, 2009, the closet has clothed an average of 750 children each year. Dozens of volunteers sort donations, get them on display shelves, and then host families as they *shop* for children's clothing.[55]

In 2010, Jacob's Closet inspired another ministry to serve St. Joseph children, *Jacob's Toy Box*. Volunteers collect donations of new toys and work with administrators at a partner school to distribute the toys just before Christmas to families in need.[56] Children at Hall Elementary School were the first beneficiaries of the Jacob's Toy Box ministry. In recent years, Jacob's Toy Box volunteers have worked with administrators at Lake Contrary Elementary School to serve families there.

Although it is true that the "mission field" is right outside the doors of the church building, in a very real sense, the mission field is also *inside* the building. People who gather at Wyatt Park need to hear the gospel, and sometimes they need help. In response to that latter need, Rev. Tommie Bouchard informed the board in 1964 about the creation of a Minister's Discretionary Fund, and that fund still exists today. Monies contributed to the fund are used by ministry staff to discreetly assist congregation members who are hurting and need help.[57]

SERVING IN LOCAL SCHOOLS

In 1991, Wyatt Park turned its attention to children in need in St. Joseph elementary schools. Organized by Ed and Vicki Christgen, the congregation provided gifts to each of the 392 children at Neely Elementary School, which is located in one of St. Joseph's economically challenged neighborhoods. In 1992, gifts were gathered for children at Webster Elementary School, also in a neighborhood that struggles economically. That effort turned into a partnership as

---

55 E-mail from Jacob's Closet coordinator Sharon Millard, filed with the board minutes, April 19, 2009.

56 *The Call to Worship*, October 5, 2010.

57 Minister's report filed with board minutes, February 10, 1964.

the congregation joined with the Webster School children to gather food dona-tions.[58] And it resulted in a partnership of a different sort by becoming a cata-lyst for a business partnership program in the St. Joseph School District.[59] The business partnership program makes it possible for businesses and churches to be supportive partners with individual elementary schools.

In response to a request from the school district, Wyatt Park formally became a partner with Lake Contrary Elementary School in 2010. "Lake" serves children in one of the most economically distressed areas of the city, and the needs are significant. During the current (2016–2017) school year, 87 percent of Lake students qualify for free or reduced lunch.[60] Since 2010, Wyatt Park members have volunteered in different ways at the school, and funds have been raised annually to underwrite student field trips and other special activities. Lake's staff has been cared for as well.

Within weeks of forming the partnership, I began the practice of going to Lake each Friday morning to pray with any staff members who wish to join for prayer. That practice continues, and since 2015 I have been joined each week by Ken Heckman, another Wyatt Park member. On at least two occa-sions, church members have donated up to $2,000 to provide each teacher with a gift card to a store selling supplies that are used by classroom teachers. The intention is to lessen the amount of their own money that Lake's teachers must use for classroom supplies.

Reminiscent of the partnership that developed with Webster School stu-dents in 1992, the partnership with Lake is two-way. Each year, Lake's stu-dents hold a "penny drive" with the proceeds going toward the Jacob's Closet clothing ministry (see above). The first penny drive was held in 2011, and afterward, Principal Jasmine Briedwell wrote to the church:

> Our student council raised $471.70 for Jacob's Closet. One morning a
> kindergartener came in the building just dragging her backpack. We

---

58 *The Call to Worship*, December 26, 1991, and November 12, 1992.

59 *The Call to Worship*, November 16, 2010.

60 Source: Author interview with Dr. Jasmine Briedwell, Principal, Lake Contrary Elementary School, May, 2017.

didn't know what was wrong because she was struggling so much… turns out she had over $12 in pennies in her bag that day! Her face lit up when we saw how much she brought in to help other children who need clothing. Thank you for allowing us to give back to you this Christmas! You have blessed our school in so many ways.[61]

Danford Hall

Multiple housing complexes for senior citizens may be found in St. Joseph today, but that is a rather recent phenomenon. Until the 1980s, housing options for older adults were limited, and local churches, including Wyatt Park, stepped forward to help meet the growing need. Actually, Wyatt Park had first considered constructing senior housing more than twenty years earlier.

In the fall of 1963, a proposal was made to consider constructing senior citizen housing near the church.[62] A committee was formed, and shortly thereafter an architect's initial drawing depicted a fourteen-story apartment building. Meetings were held and much was discussed, but by March 1964, the idea was abandoned for multiple reasons, chief among them the cost of needed real estate.[63] Twenty-two years later, the idea of constructing housing for senior citizens came up again.

In February 1986, a representative of HUD (Department of Housing and Urban Development) Community Housing met with church board members to discuss the possibility of Wyatt Park Christian Church acting as sponsor for a senior housing complex. It was recommended by the HUD representative that if the church wished to undertake the project, a separate nonprofit corporation should be formed. In terms of financial responsibilities, the congregation would only be expected to provide the land, with construction funding coming from other sources.

Land just west of the church building was deemed the most desirable building site, and a needed piece of property was for sale. After a good bit of

---

61 *The Call to Worship*, December 20, 2011.

62 Board minutes, October 14, 1963.

63 Board minutes, March 9, 1964.

discussion, the board voted to purchase the property, complete the necessary application with HUD to construct affordable housing for seniors, and take initial steps to build the facility.[64] A Housing Committee went to work but, within the first year, met with disappointment as the HUD application was turned down. However, when one door closes, another often opens.

An application was submitted to the Missouri Housing Development Commission, and it was approved in early 1987. With the approval came a deadline: ninety days to submit preliminary plans for a building. The Housing Committee had much to do. Chaired by Thad Danford, the committee also included Mel McLean, Byron Woodbury, Bob Wollenman, Shirley Chafen, Larry Hausman, and Pastor Wally Brown.[65]

As recommended at the first meeting in 1986, a nonprofit corporation was formed, WPC Housing Corporation. It became "the building and operating entity for the project," and that remains true today.[66] Support was also obtained from the National Benevolent Association, a missions arm of the Christian Church (Disciples of Christ). Meetings and planning continued, and by mid-1988, financing was secured, zoning changes were approved, and decisions were made about the size and scope of the proj-ect. It would have thirty-eight apartment units, and it would be a three-story frame building with brick trim. In addition to the apartments, there would also be a community room and laundry facilities.[67] An architect was chosen, and

---

64 Board minutes, February 17, 1986.
65 *The Call to Worship*, March 4, 1987.
66 *The Call to Worship*, September 24, 1987.
67 *St. Joseph Telegraph*, March 1, 1990.

a contract was signed with the nonprofit Community Housing Management Corporation to manage the facility. CHM still manages Danford Hall today.

Ground was broken in May 1989. As noted in the previous chapter, Housing Committee chairman Thad Danford died of a heart attack in June 1989, and in July the WPC Housing Corporation Board voted to name the facility "Danford Hall." Construction progressed, inspections were completed, and on February 23, 1990, papers were signed, officially making Danford Hall ready for occupancy. Residents began to move in immediately.[68]

Tragedy struck on Sunday, July 25, 2010, when fire broke out at about 5:00 p.m. Two residents, Ellis and Iris Stephens, died when officials believe they were overcome by smoke. The fire started when a resident went to sleep with a lit cigarette in his hand. The fire itself was confined to that resident's apartment, but smoke and water damage was extensive. Volunteers preparing for Vacation Bible School were at the church when the fire broke out, and their response was described in the church newsletter a few days later:

> The people setting up for VBS dropped what they were doing, rounded up wheel-chairs, and got shaken residents into our Social Hall. The Red Cross was summoned, and many of you came here to help when you learned of the fire. The outpouring of care and support from you and the community resulted in much hope in the midst of tragedy.[69]

All residents were forced out of their homes for several months while repairs and cleanup were completed. They began to move back into Danford Hall in December 2010.[70]

Common areas in Danford Hall were designated "no smoking" well before the tragic fire, but HUD regulations made it difficult to designate the entire facility "no smoking." Partially in response to the Danford Hall fire,

---

68 *The Call to Worship*, March 1, 1990.
69 *The Call To Worship*, August 3, 2010
70 *St. Joseph News-Press*, December 2, 2010

HUD rules were relaxed and when Danford Hall reopened, the entire facility was designated "no smoking." It remains so today.

AND FINALLY

There are approximately seven-and-a-half billion people living in the world today. While some of them live well in terms of material wealth, hundreds of millions live in extreme poverty. Millions live under the rule of oppressive regimes. Millions more are caught in the crossfire of warfare. Too many of the world's people live without hope. In other words, the need for local churches to actively and intentionally engage in missions ministries is as great as ever. Throughout its history, Wyatt Park Christian Church has done its best to carry out both sides of the call to missions: proclaiming the gospel of Jesus Christ and providing benevolent care to hurting people. Given that long history of proclamation and service, it is reasonable to expect that in the decades to come, Wyatt Park members will continue to say with the prophet Isaiah, "Here am I. Send me" (Isa. 6:8).

CHAPTER 7

Gathered to Be Effective

———

And he (Christ) is the head of the body, the church. He
is the beginning, the firstborn from the dead, that in
everything he might be preeminent. (Col. 1:18)

HUMAN BEINGS HAVE ALWAYS ORGANIZED themselves—sometimes formally,
though much of the time informally. Organizational structures that govern
most people's daily lives are simple: family, classroom, workplace, and so
forth. Societal organization is more complex of course, so much so that it
often seems to be, well, disorganized.

People of faith have organized themselves as well, and the Bible shows
how that has progressed. In the opening chapters of Genesis, people were
primarily tribal. Some lived in cities, but most lived in villages, and a few,
such as Abraham and his family, could well be described as nomads. A
few hundred years later, the Israelites were led out of slavery in Egypt and
then spent forty years in the Sinai wilderness. God formed them into a
nation, not just in terms of their religious life but in their national life as
well. Once they settled in the Promised Land (what we think of today as
Israel), the Israelites were still tribal but with more structure and organization than before. In time, they opted for a monarchy, complete with a king.
Of course, monarchies tend to attack their neighbors, and neighbors attack
them. Kings rise and fall. Kingdoms rise and fall. Israel was not immune to
any of that.

By Jesus's time, what is generally thought of as Israel was just a small part of the Roman Empire, and the Romans controlled most of the Mediterranean world. The empire featured a massive central government in Rome and a well-organized system of local and regional authorities.

There was also a highly structured system of governance at the Temple in Jerusalem in Jesus's day. He frequently criticized it because those in power had become enamored with the trappings and perks of governance but had lost sight of the purpose. Sadly, a similar critique could be made about much of the organized church throughout its history. Too often, church leaders lose sight of the truth expressed in the verse at the beginning of this chapter—*Jesus is to be the head of the church, and the church's purpose is to make and grow disciples of Jesus.*

Local congregations organize themselves in a variety of ways, and many belong to larger organizational structures usually referred to as denominations. Some congregations and denominations adopt complex, formal organizational structures. Others are less complex and formal. Wyatt Park has tended toward a structure that is simple and informal although not always. In the middle decades of the twentieth century, the congregation's structure was rather complex with boards, departments, and committees. Such were those times when institutions and their complex organizational charts were highly regarded.

GOVERNING BOARD AND GOVERNING DOCUMENTS

Exactly how Wyatt Park Christian Church was structured at the beginning is unknown. It was organized in 1888 and incorporated according to the laws of the state of Missouri in 1902, but the earliest available church board minutes are dated 1911. Board meetings in those early years often took place in board members' homes, but they were sometimes held at the church. Meeting minutes were kept in large books; penmanship was generally (although not always) much better then than it is today. Minutes tended to be concise and to the point, with little detail. There are instances when more detail would be desirable, such as this entry from November 1912: "Moved, with second, that the Chair appoint a

Toastmaster. Carried."[1] Subsequent board minutes make no further mention of it, so whether a toastmaster was appointed and what the toastmaster might have done remain unknown. More detail may not be needed, but better wording might have been nice for this entry in 1934: "Moved that House and Grounds Committee be authorized to put gas in pastor's study."[2]

Bylaws are first mentioned in August 1912 when a committee was appointed "to formulate ByLaws and rules and regulations with which to govern the business of the church."[3] The Bylaws were voted on by means of a rather laborious process in April 1913. Each of the eight Articles (sections of the Bylaws) was presented to the board, discussed, and then voted on. Once all of the articles were approved, there was this: "Moved and seconded that all rules and regulations in violation of the foregoing rules and regulations shall be null and void. Carried."[4]

Electing board officers also required a laborious process, at least in the early years, and the election in 1913 provides an illustration. The election took place within a board meeting, and as members voted on trustees, multiple ballots were needed. At one point there was a tie vote, so "It was moved and seconded that the one of the two whose name begins with the letter nearest *A* in the alphabet be declared elected for a term of three years and the other for a term of two years. Carried."[5] Since at least the mid-twentieth century, board officers have also been considered officers of the congregation, so they are elected by the congregation, not just the board. Their names are put forward by a nominating committee, first to the board and then to the congregation, and then they are voted on during the congregation's annual meetings.

Board membership has typically included elders and deacons but at times has also included trustees, department chairs, and ministry staff. Board size has fluctuated. A proposal was approved in 1936 to increase the board membership to thirty deacons and nine elders (the size of the board before that

---

1 Board minutes, November 6, 1912.
2 Board minutes, February 1934 (exact date not indicated).
3 Board minutes, August 5, 1912.
4 Board minutes, April 14, 1913.
5 Board minutes, July 7, 1913.

time is unclear). Nine years later, it was increased again to thirty-six deacons and twelve elders.[6] Boards of that size can be unwieldy, but Wyatt Park was just getting started. In 1951, a new church constitution was adopted calling for board membership of forty-eight deacons and eighteen elders. Seven years later, the congregation voted to increase board size again to its largest membership total ever: seventy-two deacons and twenty-four elders.[7] In 1960, the congregation voted on an amendment to the constitution adding deaconesses to the board. Prior to that, women were not eligible to be board members. The number of board members was tied to church membership so that there was to be one elder, one deaconess, and three deacons for every seventy-five members of the church. Board membership at a minimum would include eighteen elders, forty-eight deacons, and twelve deaconesses. The proposed amendment passed by a vote of 204-49. In an interesting newsletter article following the vote, it was noted that the pastor, Rev. Clayton Potter,

> rather marveled at the innumerable rumors going about as to what Deaconesses would do, how they would behave (or misbehave) in Board meetings, et al. Not the least of his marveling came with the news that of the 49 who cast negative votes, more than half were women![8]

Having a large number of people on the board is one thing, but getting them all to attend meetings is something else, and the latter often proved challenging. Board chairman Gerald Yurth chided his board colleagues for poor attendance in 1966, noting that while ninety-eight people were on the board, only forty-four were in attendance at the September meeting.[9]

---

6 Board minutes, August 1936 (exact date not indicated) and April 22, 1945.

7 *The Call to Worship*, May 17, 1951, March 12, 1958, and March 19, 1958. Board size was not the only unwieldy element of the constitution approved in 1951. It also listed thirty-one standing committees as well as provisions for the formation of additional committees as needed. One can only speculate about what an additional committee might have done.

8 *The Call to Worship*, January 14, 1960, and February 25, 1960.

9 Board minutes, September 12, 1966.

Board and congregation officers are elected each year, but the 1978 election of officers featured something new. Alice Purvis was elected board chair, the first time that a woman was elected to that office at Wyatt Park.[10] Even bigger changes were yet to come.

A Constitutional Revision Committee began work in the fall of 1978 to update the congregation's constitution and bylaws. An organization's governing documents should be reviewed regularly, and Wyatt Park Christian Church has done so, most of the time producing minor changes that reflect evolving circumstances. Significant revisions were proposed to the board and congregation in 1979, and they were approved.[11] The number of functional committees was consolidated to six: Worship, Membership Development, Education, Christian Service, Stewardship, and Property. Chairs of those committees would be members of a newly formed Administrative Cabinet that would oversee day-to-day operations of the church. The term "deaconess" was dropped with the board being made up of elected elders and deacons, and for the first time, women could be elected to either of those offices.[12] In 1979, Laura Ream and Barbara Crumley were elected as elders. Beulah Huss, Alice Sawyer, Sue Shearer, and Beverly Shipley were elected as deacons.[13] It would be another thirty years before governing documents again underwent major revision.

At the start of the twenty-first century, organizations of all kinds were discovering that structures which worked well in the 1950s did not work well in a new century. Organizational structures were streamlined to make them more efficient and flexible. Wyatt Park joined that trend when the church board approved an overhaul of the bylaws at its first meeting in 2009. Under the new bylaws, the board, which had been comprised of nearly seventy people, was reduced to thirteen, plus three ministry staff. Elders and deacons no longer automatically serve on the board. Instead, each group selects individuals to represent them on the board. And, unlike earlier bylaws, the new documents did not name teams or committees, "because the church's needs are

---

10 *The Call to Worship*, June 22, 1978.

11 *The Call to Worship*, May 10, 1979.

12 Constitution and Bylaws, adopted by congregational vote, May 6, 1979.

13 Election ballot, filed with Called Congregational Meeting Minutes, May 6, 1979.

continually changing, and that means the need for teams and committees is also continually changing."[14] That means, of course, that Wyatt Park's governing documents will undergo another revision at some time in the future, which is as it should be.

ELDERS AND DEACONS

Throughout most of Wyatt Park's history, all elders and deacons served on the church board, but each position involved more than monthly board meetings. Elders and deacons have two important, but distinct, roles in the life of the church. Both offices have a scriptural foundation, and when they are lived out according to the biblical descriptions, elders and deacons are essential to the spiritual health of a congregation and its individual members. In April 1964, *The Call to Worship* published extended articles about the offices of elder and deacon. Although published more than fifty years ago, the content of the articles is timeless, and excerpts are shared here—beginning with the office of elder. Note that when these articles were published, only men could serve as elders and deacons, and the writing reflects that limitation:

> The Elders of the Church are selected on the basis of their ability to bring wisdom to the ministry of the Church. Usually they are older men, but at no place in the New Testament is there any suggested age of eligibility. The main emphasis is upon the man's ability to give wise counsel and leadership to the fellowship of believers. The prime consideration is not age but spiritual maturity.
>
> In the New Testament Elders are known variously as Elders, Overseers, Bishops, Teachers, and Pastors. These titles suggest their varied responsibilities. As Elders they are to be a source of wisdom. As Bishops or Overseers it is their responsibility to watch over and superintend the spiritual development of the congregation. They are called Pastors or Shepherds because they are required to have a shepherd's

---

14 *The Call to Worship*, January 20, 2009, and board minutes, January 19, 2009.

concern and care for the flock; to lead souls to the Good Shepherd. Their teaching role calls them to teach all who are under their care the laws and love of God.

Such a description of the office of Elder might very well frighten those who are thus called to serve. No man can do all of this. Yet, in the harmony of Christian love and devotion to increased measures of perfection, the Elders are sustained by the grace of God. As a group they share in the spiritual leadership of the Church. As individuals they work to show themselves approved of God as good stewards of His word.[15]

Service at the communion table is the most visible role of elders at Wyatt Park. During traditional worship, that role consists of prayers for the bread, cup, and offering. Increasingly, elders are presiding at the Lord's Supper during the praise-style worship services as well.

One week later, an extended article was published about deacons, and it included these excerpts:

The word deacon comes from a Greek word which means "active service." The New Testament calls for the deacons to be selected from men of good reputation who have both a practical bent and a spiritual outlook. Their role was different from that of the elders; but no less important. While the elders were responsible for teaching, the deacons were called to look after the affairs of the functioning church.

Just what were these functions? It started out as a means to look after the widows of the church who needed help. But soon the responsibilities grew until the deacons became responsible for other secular needs which had to be met by the Church. They kept books, handled financial affairs, looked after properties, and worked among the congregation as active ministers or servants. In all of this they were expected to bring a spiritual concern to their work.[16]

---

15 *The Call to Worship*, April 23, 1964.
16 *The Call to Worship*, April 30, 1964.

As with the elders, service at the communion table during the traditional worship service is the most visible role of deacons at Wyatt Park. Deacons distribute the communion elements and pass the offering plates. Of course, since the word "deacon" means "active service," deacons may be found serving in almost every capacity around the church.

The 1964 articles concluded with an important reminder about the significance of both elders and deacons:

> It should also be noted that the difference between Elders and Deacons is not a matter of rank; but of function. The Apostle Paul pointed out that all are members of the same body and therefore none can say to the other "I have no need of you" or that, "I am better or more important than you." For, in fact, the work and mission of the Church can be fulfilled only when there is a balanced division of labor and responsibility. No person and no group can provide the total ministry. Thus, each has an important role of service to render, without which the total Church suffers.[17]

JUNIOR BOARD

For more than a decade beginning in 1947, there was another board at Wyatt Park, the Junior Board. Its purpose was "cooperating with and assisting the Senior Board, in handling activities of the church assigned by the Senior Board (the Church Board)."[18] No doubt there was plenty to do, but the congregation faced another challenge—enviable, but still a challenge—that was mentioned in a newsletter article just before the annual election in June 1947. It listed those being nominated for elder and deacon and then noted:

> The names already on the ballot are those nominated by the Official Board from a much larger list of men. Wyatt Park Christian Church

---

17 Ibid.

18 Bylaws, Junior Board, Wyatt Park Christian Church. Approved by the Senior Board, November 3, 1947.

is embarrassed with a wealth of manpower. We wish it were possible for many other men to be elected to the Board as there are many who are well qualified. But until the Board is enlarged, only this number can be elected.[19]

Although the sense of being "embarrassed with a wealth of manpower" may not have been widely felt, clearly the congregation needed to find ways to enable more young men to become actively engaged in the ministries of the church. The formation of a Junior Board provided at least a partial answer. The Junior Board nominated and elected its own members and officers, with approval from the Senior Board. Initial Junior Board membership was limited to thirty men, but that number fluctuated a bit in the years that followed. Once organized, a newsletter article noted the number of men in service and leadership at Wyatt Park:

The Junior Board is composed of thirty young men, ranging in age from about 24 to 45. The Board was formed to give an opportunity for service and leadership to the growing group of younger men in the church. With the 50 men now on the Senior Board, we have 80 men who hold responsibility in the on-going life of the church.[20]

Junior Board members served as ushers for weekly worship services and oversaw church athletic leagues. Members were active in the early years, but by the early 1960s, Junior Board membership and participation had declined considerably. While it is unclear when the Junior Board disbanded, the latest document pertaining to the Junior Board is dated September 1961.[21]

DOLLARS AND CENTS

For many people, organizational budgeting and finance makes for rather dull reading, but the way an organization develops spending plans and

---

19 *The Call to Worship*, June 26, 1947.

20 *The Call to Worship*, November 27, 1947.

21 Junior Board report, September 18, 1961, contained in "Junior Board" file folder.

manages financial resources can provide insight into its purpose and priorities. Interesting tidbits may be found as well.

Budgets for Wyatt Park's earliest years are not available. The earliest annual budget that has been found is for the year 1919. It totaled $3,300, with another $445 designated for missions spending. Of the $3,300 budgeted for the year, over half, $1,800, went toward the pastor's annual salary.[22] Paying the pastor in a timely way had proven difficult just five years earlier.

J. M. Asbell was called to be Wyatt Park's pastor in November, 1911, at an annual compensation of $1,400.[23] Within two years, the congregation found itself three months behind in paying his salary. Board members instructed the Finance Committee to "spare no efforts" in collecting money pledged to pay him what was owed.[24] Some progress was made in the months that followed, but by April 1914, the amount of back pay owed to Brother Asbell ("Brother" was a common way to refer to pastors in those days) was again equivalent to almost three months' salary. In the meantime, other expenditures were discussed and approved at that April board meeting. Board members instructed the House and Grounds Committee to work with the Ladies Aid Society to develop renovation plans for the entrance to the church. And the meeting minutes also note, "Moved and seconded that the cash collections for the next four Sundays be used for the purchase of new song books."[25] It should not have been a surprise when, six days later, Brother Asbell submitted his resignation. He was persuaded by the board to withdraw his resignation the next day.[26]

Financial collections continued to be a problem, and in June 1914, the board voted to take what today would be considered a very drastic step:

> Moved and seconded that the Finance Committee make a financial statement of the church showing the names of all members, amount subscribed, amount paid, balance due, etc. Also showing the entire

---

22 Board minutes, December 2, 1918.
23 Board minutes, November 21, 1911.
24 Board minutes, September 8, 1913.
25 Board minutes, April 6, 1914.
26 Board minutes, April 12, 1914, and April 13, 1914.

indebtedness of the church in detail, and to deliver a copy of said statement to each member or family. Motion unanimously carried.[27]

In other words, each church member would know what every church member had pledged, paid to date, and still owed. Such an action would be unheard of today, but it was done, and the Finance Committee reported at the next meeting that "some back debts have since been paid."[28] Still, the primary catalyst for that action remained unresolved, and by November, the back pay owed the pastor amounted to more than four months' salary. He resigned again, and that time it was accepted. The board passed a resolution commending Brother Asbell for his service and also gave the Finance Committee some more instructions:

> The Finance Committee is instructed to make lists of all subscribing members, distribute them among Board members who are to see these people and ask them to pay their entire 1914 pledges, and as much more as they can by Sunday, the 15th, in order that we may pay Brother Asbell his back salary of about $500.[29]

That effort met with some success, and by the end of the month, the pastor had been paid about half of what he was owed. It is unclear from subsequent meeting minutes whether the full amount was ever paid, although the board did continue extra efforts to collect pledges and the like, so it would be reasonable to assume that the congregation eventually honored its financial commitment to Brother Asbell.

Through the years since then, the congregation has had little trouble meeting its financial obligations, at least *most* of the time. There were times when difficult decisions had to be made. Such was the case during the Great Depression when salaries were repeatedly cut or eliminated and other expense reduction measures were taken. For example, in 1933, the board voted to allow

---

27 Board minutes, June 8, 1914.

28 Board minutes, July 6, 1914.

29 Board minutes, November 2, 1914.

the building to be open only on Fridays and Sundays, as a way to save money.[30] As noted in chapters 2 and 5, World War II took a toll on the congregation in many ways, including financial support. Once the war was over, Wyatt Park's financial picture brightened considerably. Rev. Lawrence Bash noted the congregation's financial growth in a March 1947 newsletter column:

> In four short years, our budget has grown from $7,200 to $26,626, almost quadrupled. A substantial part of the gain goes to missions which increases from $600 to $10,000. That is as it should be.[31]

The $10,000 for missions was included within the total of $26,626, meaning that in 1947, 37 percent of Wyatt Park's budget went toward missions. By compassion, missions giving today averages 10–12 percent of all dollars flowing through the church. Part of that amount is given through Designated Funds, an option that was unavailable in 1947.

A year later the tone of Rev. Bash's message to the congregation had changed as the congregation approached another day of pledging financial commitment to the church:

> As your minister, there are two things I have in mind as we approach this day of Dedication. The first is the disturbing fact that many people hold membership in this church, yet give it no support financially. The church would die in one year were all members of this mind. My second hope is that all of us shall show evidence of "growing in grace" this year. The Christian life can never be static, motionless. This should be reflected in our giving. Why not move up to the tithe this year? Have you ever bothered to calculate the percentage of your net income that you contribute? Make a study of it this week. Are you giving in such a way that it could honestly be called "Christian?" The future program of the church depends on you.[32]

---

30 Board minutes, November 1933 (exact date is not indicated).
31 *The Call to Worship*, March 6, 1947.
32 *The Call to Worship*, February 26, 1948.

His message was effective because it was reported in the next newsletter that sixty-five people had committed to tithe (giving one-tenth of their income).

A new way to financially support the church was created in 1950 with the establishment of the Abiding Memorials Fund, which still exists today. It is a "fund to which contributions may be made in memory of any person. The amount of the gift may be of any size."[33] Proceeds from the fund are used for worship and/or facility enhancement.

Throughout much of Wyatt Park's history, financial campaigns were an annual ritual. Volunteers called on church members, and everyone was encouraged to make a financial pledge to support the congregation's ministry in the upcoming year. Some of the pledge campaigns were huge affairs with dinners and as many as two hundred volunteers.[34] Although campaigns often encouraged people to pledge toward a proposed church budget, 1961 campaign chairman Herb Woodbury made it clear that pledging to a budget was not the point:

> Our concern is that every member of the church pledge to the program of the church because he wants to do so. We will not be pledging to a proposed budget this year, although one is available for those who want to see it. We will pledge to God and the work of His church out of love for Him.[35]

The concept that "we will pledge to God and the work of His church out of love for Him" came into fullness in the early 2000s when Wyatt Park stopped conducting pledge campaigns toward the operating budget. For two years, members were given pledge cards and encouraged to prayerfully consider the amount they would give, write it down, and then keep the card as a reminder of their commitment to God. Pledge cards were not to be turned in to the church. By 2005, even that remnant of operating budget pledge campaigns had come to an end. Since that time, some years have ended with

---

33 *The Call to Worship*, January 11, 1956.

34 *The Call to Worship*, November 20, 1952, February 19, 1953, and January 28, 1954.

35 *The Call to Worship*, October 26, 1961.

small deficits, and some have ended with small surpluses. Through it all, God has proven faithful, providing the resources needed to carry on the ministry of Wyatt Park Christian Church. Wyatt Park does seek financial pledges for periodic capital campaigns that are used to underwrite major facility repair and improvement projects.

KEEPING TRACK OF IT ALL

Although a local congregation's primary purpose is ministry, there is a financial side that must be diligently attended to. For much of Wyatt Park's history, that was directed by the Finance Committee with support from church office staff. In 1965, the church board voted to employ Willis Hintz as Church Administrator. A newsletter article noted that he would oversee administrative functions throughout the church, with emphasis on the Stewardship, Property, and Evangelism departments:

> In the action Monday night the board brought to reality a long sustained dream to have a specialist in administration in order to free the ministerial staff for the unique services they have to render in behalf of the congregation.[36]

Willis Hintz joined the church staff following a career in the military, but his tenure at Wyatt Park was short lived. Because of a decrease in the church's financial resources, he resigned in January 1966. The church treasurer and other volunteers worked with church office staff to oversee finances until 1988.

Meryldee Buckner joined the church staff in June 1988 as Financial Secretary. Her title was changed to Business Manager in the mid-1990s, and she remained in that position until her retirement in June 2009. She handled all of the business and financial responsibilities and saw her work as

---

36 *The Call to Worship*, April 15, 1965.

ministry. When her retirement was announced, an important benefit of her twenty-one-year tenure was noted in the newsletter:

> After 21 years, Meryldee knows you well and her deep knowledge of the people of Wyatt Park will be missed. As someone said during a recent Board meeting, "We are not only losing a business manager—we're losing an archive."[37]

The Social Hall was full on June 10 for her retirement dinner. She wrote a thank-you note to the congregation illustrating how she saw her work as ministry. She noted the different speakers at the dinner and then said, "But I'm probably proudest that Phillip Walters spoke recalling our days of Sunday School and church camp" (Phillip Walters grew up at Wyatt Park and was in her Sunday-School class and also at church camp where she served as a counselor).[38] She remains an active member of the church and returned to the staff for a few months as Interim Business Manager in August 2012.

Pam West was hired as the new Business Manager in June 2009. She brought exceptional skills to the job, but she also brought something else, and it resulted in one of the most painful periods in Wyatt Park's history. During all three worship services on August 18–19, 2012, the following statement was shared with the congregation:

> Last weekend (8/11–12), we received information that there might be an accounting issue that needed to be examined in the business office of the church. On Monday morning (8/13), a group of church leaders met to develop a plan of action. That plan called for us to immediately conduct an internal audit.
>
> We felt that it was necessary to conduct this audit without the assistance of our Business Manager. As such, we met with the Business

---

37 *The Call to Worship*, April 7, 2009.
38 *The Call to Worship*, June 16, 2009.

Manager on Monday afternoon and advised her that we would be placing her on paid leave through the rest of the week.

The initial audit revealed a number of areas of concern. This included several unauthorized expenditures and forged signatures. In short, we believed that church money was used for individual purposes that were not authorized. We believe that this action was the conduct of a single individual. That individual's employment with the church was terminated this week (week of 8/13).

Due to the nature of this discovery, we notified the St. Joseph Police Department and they are investigating. We have also initiated a claim with our insurance carrier, and it is believed that these amounts will most likely be recoverable under our church insurance policy. As to the future, we will be taking steps to institute additional safeguards that will reduce the risk of this happening again.[39]

As noted above, former Business Manager Meryldee Buckner returned to the position on an interim basis following the Board action terminating Ms. West, who was arrested on August 27, 2012, and charged with Class C felony stealing.[40] Church treasurer Nancy Wheatley spent more than a month going through countless files and the business manager's computer. It was determined that for nearly three years, Ms. West had carefully manipulated accounts and created fake accounts. In addition, she forged checks and successfully hid them from monthly reports provided to the board. It was determined that over the course of the three years, she had stolen $86,000 from the church. She entered a guilty plea on November 15, 2012, and on January 24, 2013, was sentenced to the maximum seven years in prison.[41] One week later, an informational meeting was held in the Social Hall to explain in detail what she did, how she did it, and what steps were taken to reduce the risk of it happening again.

---

39 *The Call to Worship*, August 28, 2012.
40 *St. Joseph News-Press*, August 28, 2012.
41 *St. Joseph News-Press*, January 24, 2013.

After serving 120 days in prison, Ms. West was put on probation and ordered to make restitution payments to cover the amount over and above the $50,000 that the church received from the insurance claim. Those restitution payments continue to be made.

A congregation's true character comes out during such an event. Two pastor's columns in the newsletter describe how the congregation responded, revealing something of its character. The first appeared August 28, 2012, when the statement to the congregation was published:

> We do not intend to allow this violation of trust to change who we are. We are a loving, caring, trusting, Christ-centered congregation. I (author) have been deeply touched by the evidence of love and support as this church family has pulled together. And, there is something that I believe speaks volumes about the "heart condition" of Wyatt Park, and that is the number of you who have said you are praying for our former Business Manager. You are not praying that she get out of facing any consequences for her actions, but you are praying that God will help her find healing and that she can eventually rebuild her life.[42]

The second column was published following the January 2013 informational meeting. It included these excerpts:

> On Wednesday evening, January 30th, the Social Hall was full as Treasurer Nancy Wheatley and Finance Team Chair Bud Salanski shared information about the stealing that was discovered in our business office last August.
>
> In a situation that could have been filled with anger, hurtful words, and finger-pointing, instead what has been experienced throughout this whole ordeal is love, grace, and a desire for healing. For Pam, that means a desire that she will be able to turn her life around. For us, it

---

42 *The Call to Worship*, August 28, 2012.

has meant admitting our mistakes and making procedural changes that will greatly reduce the risk of this kind of thing happening again.

Such a thing could turn ugly in some churches, but not here. You all continue to demonstrate—*regularly*—the love and grace of our Savior Jesus Christ.[43]

In September 2012, the board approved a proposal to fill the Business Manager position and also change it. Peggy Verbick had joined the Wyatt Park staff as part-time Communications Secretary in December 1997. The board approved combining her position with that of Business Manager into one, full-time Office Manager position; she still holds that title today.

In 2015, Wyatt Park Christian Church took an additional step toward stronger administration with the calling of Cindy Crouse as Administrative Pastor. That new position is similar to what had been intended in 1965 with the hiring of Willis Hintz. Ms. Crouse had previously worked in public education where she spent many years as a counselor and then as an administrator overseeing the counseling staff of the St. Joseph School District. She came to Wyatt Park to "guide the administrative and organizational side of our various ministries. She will also assist with some pastoral duties, especially in the areas of counseling and individual pastoral care."[44] Since joining the staff, she has added responsibilities that include counseling, teaching classes and assisting in worship.

ONE BODY, MANY PARTS

As noted in the opening chapter, Wyatt Park Christian Church is associated with the Christian Church (Disciples of Christ), one of three denominations that trace their roots to a nineteenth-century reform movement led by Thomas and Alexander Campbell and also Barton Stone. The denomination is congregational in structure, meaning that each congregation is essentially

---

43 *The Call to Worship*, February 12, 2013.
44 *The Call to Worship*, June 24, 2014.

independent and denominational participation is voluntary. The denomination does not own any local church property, so the Wyatt Park Christian Church property is held in the name of the congregation's trustees. The congregation is free to call whomever it chooses to fill ministry positions. Through the twentieth century, those positions were generally filled through the Disciples of Christ Search and Call system, but the pool of qualified candidates has diminished in recent years. Most ministry staff positions since 2000 have been filled from outside the denomination. Financial contributions to the Disciples of Christ are voluntary, and Wyatt Park has contributed to the denomination throughout the congregation's history.

While financial support continues, the Wyatt Park Christian Church Board voted in 2005 to keep denominational contributions within Missouri, because the congregation has long seen part of its mission as being one of providing support to smaller churches in outlying communities. Toward that end, on many occasions Wyatt Park has brought teachers and church leaders to St. Joseph, making them available to pastors and local church leaders from throughout northwest Missouri. Today, Wyatt Park's primary connections with the Disciples of Christ are through women's ministries, the summer camping program, and some mentoring that I do with new pastors in northwest Missouri.

Denominational participation peaked in the middle decades of the twentieth century. Pastors and church members were regularly involved in state and national conventions and other activities. It was a time when regard for institutions was high and most denominational institutions were thriving. The list of working committees and programming options was impressive, and statewide gatherings routinely attracted large crowds. One example is the 1957 state convention that was held in St. Joseph at First Christian Church. More than one thousand delegates attended. During the weekend, they worshiped; listened to multiple guest speakers; approved a new constitution for the Christian Churches in Missouri; participated in men's, women's, and youth events; and attended multiple workshops.[45]

---

45 *The Call to Worship*, May 8, 1957.

Wyatt Park Christian Church hosted a similar gathering in 2004. By then, the Christian Churches of Missouri was known by its current name, "the Christian Church in Mid-America." The Mid-America region includes all of Missouri outside of Kansas City, plus three Illinois counties that are part of metropolitan St. Louis. The regional assembly format was similar to earlier gatherings with worship, business meetings, workshops, and so forth. Registration totaled 350 people.[46]

In the early 1960s, the Disciples of Christ began an effort to restructure itself, and the multiyear process was guided by a 120-member Commission on Restructure of the Christian Church Brotherhood. The commission was made up of ministers and church members ("laymen" was the term then), and one of those commission members was Wyatt Park's pastor at the time, Rev. Tommie Bouchard. Prior to one of the commission's four-day meetings, the purpose of their work was described in *The Call to Worship*:

> The ultimate plan of this commission is to develop a new structure wherein God's will can be more fully realized through our Brotherhood, and unity achieved, in response to Jesus' command that the church should be ONE.[47]

When the Disciples of Christ gathered for their international convention in 1968, delegates voted on the proposed restructure of the denomination. The convention was held in Kansas City, and Wyatt Park Christian Church was well represented. Delegates from the congregation were Herbert Woodbury, William Smith, Charles Salanski, Laura Ream, Associate Pastor Richard Tarr, Leland Becraft, Dr. Gerald Yurth, and Clyde Keely.[48]

Delegates approved a proposed Design of the Christian Church (Disciples of Christ). There has been resistance to calling the document a "constitution," but that, in essence, is what it is. "The Design" is a twenty-page governing document that describes how the denomination is structured and functions.

---

46 *The Call to Worship*, October 18, 2004.
47 *The Call to Worship*, June 27, 1963.
48 *The Call to Worship*, August 29, 1968.

Christian unity may have been the stated goal of the restructure process, but unity was not the outcome. In the months before and immediately after the convention in Kansas City, some three thousand congregations formally withdrew from the Disciples of Christ.[49] Many withdrew because of theological differences, while others withdrew because of concern about the threat of greater denominational control over local congregations as a result of the restructure. Concerns about increased denominational control were unfounded.

Like other "mainline" denominations, the Christian Church (Disciples of Christ) has seen a steady decline in membership and participation in recent decades.[50] St. Joseph illustrates that trend. There were six Disciples of Christ congregations in St. Joseph in the mid-twentieth century, but there are only three congregations in the city today: Wyatt Park Christian Church, First Christian Church, and Woodson Chapel Christian Church. Of the other three congregations, Central Christian Church (formerly known as Frederick Avenue Christian Church) and King Hill Christian Church withdrew from the denomination, while Mitchell Park Christian Church closed.

STUDIED AND STUDIED AGAIN

Healthy organizations periodically look at themselves to identify strengths upon which to build, problems needing to be fixed, opportunities that should be pursued, and challenges that must be faced. Wyatt Park Christian Church has examined itself several times—sometimes internally and sometimes by bringing in an outside observer. Many of the studies have dealt with facility needs, while some have focused on programming. Occasionally, there were studies conducted by outside consultants, intended to assess the underlying health of the congregation. One of those outside consultants was Lyle

---

49 http://disciples.org/our-identity/history-of-the-disciples/, accessed June 5, 2017.

50 A comparison of membership and the number of churches will suffice to illustrate the trend. In 1966, before restructure, there were 1,061,844 participating members in 8,066 churches across the United States. In 2015, there were 273,966 participating members in 3,308 churches. Sources: *1967 Yearbook of the Christian Churches (Disciples of Christ)* and *2016 Yearbook and Directory*, Christian Church (Disciples of Christ).

Schaller, a sociologist, ordained pastor, and consultant to the Christian Church (Disciples of Christ). He was described in *The Call to Worship* as "the most sought after authority on congregational dynamics in the nation."[51] He came to Wyatt Park as a consultant in 1978 and again in 1983.

During three days at Wyatt Park in October 1978, Mr. Schaller interviewed 139 people. His organization studied reports and statistical data about the congregation that were compiled prior to his arrival. He also gathered data about surrounding churches and the city of St. Joseph. In late October, he submitted his report titled "A New Generation?" The title was taken from the youth chorus "The New Generation Singers" (see chapter 3). In a letter introducing the report, Mr. Schaller noted the strength of the New Generation Singers and also many other strong points, including study groups and SHARE groups, an active Stewardship Department, new young adult leaders, committed Sunday-School teachers, and a beautiful sanctuary. However, there was another side to the story, and it was the reason for the question mark at the end of report's title:

> The fame of the New Generation Singers allows most of the adults at WPCC to passively bask in the reflected glory of this huge youth group. During the eight years this singing group has flourished at WPCC, average attendance has dropped, the level of financial support has not even kept pace with the increase in the general price level, the adult choir has dwindled in size, the number of participating members has shrunk, more members transferred out than transferred in, the ministry to the under-35 age bracket has declined, the CWF has dwindled, the median age of the membership has increased, the number of adult new members being received, assimilated and accepted into leadership positions decreased, Sunday School attendance dropped by one-third, the number of baptisms dropped by nearly fifty percent, and the number of contributing members decreased.[52]

---

51 *The Call to Worship*, October 5, 1978.
52 Yokefellow Institute, "A New Generation?" October 25, 1978.

He wrote that Wyatt Park experienced what many other churches had discovered, namely, "A strong youth program is not the way to insure the vitality and future growth of a congregation."[53] Ten specific recommendations were included in the report, all intended to strengthen ministries of the church beyond just the New Generation Singers.

Lyle Schaller returned to Wyatt Park in April 1983, and his methodology was similar to what was employed in 1978—statistical analysis, observations, and interviews with congregation members. The report titled "How Will You Vote?" was built around the theme of a "central question," and the title was based on how congregational leadership might "vote" on ten specific questions, all related to the central question. It suggested that the central question could be stated in two different ways. One way to state it would be this: "Would you like to see WPCC concentrate a large proportion of all of its resources on reaching the generation of parents born after 1945?" In other words, should resources be focused on attracting young families? He wrote that the overwhelming answer would likely be "yes," but he also noted that "it might be a largely passive support." Mr. Schaller suggested a better way to word the central question would be, "Are you willing to accept and actively affirm the changes that may be necessary if WPCC is going to reach, attract, serve, and assimilate this younger generation of parents?" Interestingly, the paragraphs about the "central question" were preceded by ten observations about recent changes in the life of the church. The first four were positive observations, and each of them was related to attracting young families. "How Will You Vote?" concluded with warnings about what might happen if church leaders voted no, followed by three pages of suggestions about how they might move forward if they voted yes.[54]

After the report was presented to the board, a Schaller Study Committee was formed to examine his observations and conclusions in depth and then make recommendations. It was a large group, twenty-five members plus Senior Pastor Wally Brown and Associate Pastor Bill McCutchen, who both participated ex officio (without vote). Each committee member was assigned

---

53 Ibid.
54 Yokefellow Institute, "How Will You Vote?" April 23, 1983.

to one of two teams: a team for the affirmative and a team for the negative.[55] Based on the committee's eventual recommendations, negative reactions to the Schaller report prevailed.

Although the report included useful information, there were questions about its statistical analysis, especially with regard to characteristics of St. Joseph's population when compared to nationwide data. A lack of continuity with the 1978 Schaller report was noted, as was a glaring omission from the 1983 study. It made no mention at all of the 1980 departure of the New Generation Singers, the impact their leaving had on the congregation, or the steps that had been taken to move beyond that sad event.[56]

Ultimately, the study committee concluded that the central question facing Wyatt Park Christian Church was not how to attract people of a particular age group. Rather, it was, "Can we design and implement a program to develop the needed leaders?"[57] Creation of a leadership development program was the top priority among four proposals made by the committee, and all of the committee's proposals were approved by the board.[58]

Another extensive study was conducted five years later, this time by the Northwest Area of the Christian Church (Disciples of Christ). Similar to the five-year time span between the two reports from Lyle Schaller, a significant event impacted the congregation during the five-year time span between the second Schaller report and the denominational study. In 1980, the New Generation Singers left Wyatt Park, and their departure left deep wounds. In 1987, Rev. Wally Brown left the church. He was one of the principle players in the drama surrounding the departure of New-G, and his leaving in 1987 was accompanied by ill feelings. As noted in the 1988 study, "The New Generation conflict has not gone away."[59]

Unlike the Schaller reports that included multiple recommendations, the 1988 study consisted of an extensive survey of the congregation along with

---

55 Meeting minutes, Schaller Study Committee, July 17, 1983.

56 "Position Statement: Schaller Study Committee Team for the Negative Response," Summer 1983.

57 Meeting minutes, Schaller Study Committee, August 21, 1983.

58 Board minutes, September 19, 1983.

59 Congregational Studies of Wyatt Park Christian Church, 1988, p. 17.

summaries of the findings. It made no recommendations, leaving it to congregational leaders to consider the findings and then develop an action plan. Two interviewers conducted the study and shared their impressions. In general, they found not only a congregation with great potential but also some deep wounds and no clear sense of vision or mission. They both found a genuine desire for spiritual growth and a greater emphasis on the Bible during worship. Wyatt Park was observed to be a hurting congregation, but also one with underlying strength and a continuing commitment of its people.[60]

Twenty years later, in 2008, the ministry staff and a dozen of the congregation's elected leaders spent a few months engaged in a Spiritual Strategic Journey. The goal was not to find out what church members might desire for Wyatt Park Christian Church over the next three to five years, but rather it was to discern what *God* desired for the congregation. Former church board moderator Robin McLean, by then living in Kansas City, facilitated the group's discussions. It was "spiritual" because it was centered on God and His will; "strategic" because it looked ahead three to five years; and a "journey" because when it comes to one's spiritual life, "getting there" can be almost as important as the destination.

In the end, the group discerned that God was calling the congregation to focus on helping people go deeper in their walk with Jesus. Three words beginning with the letter *E* were helpful in explaining what the group believed God was calling the congregation to focus on:

Engagement—enabling you to become more deeply engaged with God and with one another. The goal is deepened, meaningful relationships.

Equipping—enabling you to live out your engagement with God and others by helping you identify your God-given gifts and talents, and then preparing (equipping) you to use those gifts in ways that honor God.

Effectiveness—intentionally measuring what we are doing so we know whether or not it works.[61]

---

60 Congregational Studies of Wyatt Park Christian Church, 1988, pp. 21–22.
61 *The Call to Worship*, October 12, 2008.

Progress has been made since then in applying the three Es to Wyatt Park's ministries, but more remains to be done so the "journey" continues.

THE CALL TO WORSHIP

Good communication is an essential ingredient for healthy organizations. In a local church, members and potential members need to be regularly informed about events, opportunities, needs, and the "what," "how," and "why" of decision making.

Worship services provide a weekly opportunity to communicate because much of the congregation is gathered together, but there are limits to how many announcements people will welcome during those times. Worship bulletins are good tools for communication because most people use them during worship and then they take them home. Phone calls are useful, and letters and fliers may be sent by mail. Strategically placed bulletin boards are helpful if they are regularly updated. These days, much communication is done electronically via e-mail, Wyatt Park's Facebook page and Instagram account, and the congregation's website, wyattparkcc.org. And, of course, there is the newsletter, *The Call to Worship*. For several decades, it was the primary means of communication at Wyatt Park, and it still functions that way for many in the congregation.

The *Call to Worship* began weekly publication on October 10, 1946. Prior to that, simple newsletters were occasionally published, but worship bulletins were the primary printed method of communication at Wyatt Park. For the first twenty-two years of publication, *The Call to Worship* was professionally printed with the cost underwritten by donors and, at least in the beginning years, a subscription price of fifty cents per year.[62] During those early years, the newsletter was published weekly, except during the summer months when it was published monthly, or not at all. By the mid-1950s, *The Call to Worship* was published weekly throughout the year. Something else about the newsletter had changed by the mid-1950s. While still an important way to publicize

---

62 *The Call to Worship*, October 10, 1946.

upcoming activities, it began to regularly feature lengthier, more in-depth articles about matters of faith and church life. In early 1969, the appearance of the newsletter changed dramatically. Instead of being professionally printed, the newsletter was printed "in house," and that is still the case today.[63] In the early years of in-house printing, the appearance was limited to what could be done on a typewriter, but advances in computer technology and desktop publishing software have enabled the newsletter's *look* to evolve. Today, it is a multipage, multicolor publication that includes photos, graphics, and text.

As noted above, multiple electronic methods of communication are used today, and although the newsletter is still important, its role has diminished somewhat. In response to changing communication preferences by church members, and increased mailing costs, the newsletter transitioned to two issues per month in 2007, and it became a monthly publication in December 2016.[64]

Since its beginning, *The Call to Worship* has generally featured columns by the pastor(s). Many "pastor's columns" have dealt with church events, either upcoming or recently passed. Several have been used to teach something about scripture, the church, or living as a follower of Jesus. A few have addressed painful moments in human history—locally and beyond.

In October 1953, Rev. Tom Toler reflected on the grisly discovery of a child's body in a shallow grave behind a house on south Thirty-Eighth Street, near Mitchell Avenue. It was the body of six-year-old Bobby Greenlease, whose father was a prominent car dealer in Kansas City. The child had been kidnapped and then murdered by two drug addicts. Rev. Toler wrote about the Greenlease case in particular but then went on to note that:

> there are many places on the face of the earth where the death of a child is no shocking event. It is an every-day occurrence. Who can hear the description of the streets of India and other places, and not be touched by the plaintive cry of little children, "No mama, no papa,

63 *The Call to Worship*, February 13, 1969.
64 Cabinet minutes, March 19, 2007, and *The Call to Worship*, November 22, 2016.

no money." Who is not moved to know that hundreds of little children as well as adults starve to death in the streets of the world every day and night?[65]

Ten years later, in September 1963, Rev. Tommie Bouchard reflected on the deaths of four black children who were attending Sunday School at the Sixteenth Street Baptist Church in Birmingham, Alabama. They died when ten sticks of dynamite exploded. Rev. Bouchard noted, "By sheer chance of birth they were Negroes. This week they are casualties in their race's struggle to win their birthright as free people in a free nation." He went on to lament that some advocate racial segregation on biblical grounds, which is only possible through a horrible misreading of scripture.[66]

In the midst of the 1967 Six-Day War between Israel and some of its Arab neighbors, Rev. Loyal Northcott urged restraint when it comes to second-guessing the decisions of our leaders. He wrote thus:

> There is a vast step between our little soap boxes and the president's chair where final responsibility rests. As citizens, we need to study carefully the issues and express our conclusions in the right way. But even more we need to be much in prayer for the leaders of the nations in these days.[67]

On April 20, 1999, two students at Columbine High School outside Denver shocked the nation as they murdered twelve classmates and one teacher, wounded twenty more people, and then took their own lives. That same week, the Billy Graham Association held the Heartland Celebration in St. Joseph. I wrote about the contrasting images and their stark reminder of the difference between turning away from God and turning toward Him:

---

65 *The Call to Worship*, October 15, 1953.
66 *The Call to Worship*, September 19, 1963.
67 *The Call to Worship*, June 8, 1967.

It was a week of extremes. Last Tuesday, we were all horrified as we watched the chilling scenes from Littleton, Colorado. Hundreds of students poured out of a high school in fear, trying to get away from gunfire and exploding bombs. Then on Saturday evening, I was blessed with the opportunity to witness hundreds of students pouring onto the field at Spratt Stadium; not in fear, but in joyous submission to Jesus Christ. Youth Night at the Heartland Celebration could not have come at a better time. We all needed the healing it offered.[68]

On September 11, 2001, Islamist terrorists struck the United States, crashing passenger planes into both towers of the World Trade Center in New York and the Pentagon outside Washington, DC. A fourth plane crashed in rural Pennsylvania when passengers foiled the terrorists' attack plans. More than three thousand people were killed. The next day, Dr. Gene Mockabee wrote of the horrific events from the day before: "When such tragedy strikes there are no words adequate for our anguish, sorrow, anger, and fear." He then went on to quote Psalm 119:1–10, which ends with the words "I am greatly afflicted." Then he added, "It is important now to keep the faith, even when we are greatly afflicted. May God comfort you and yours. We must meet to pray this Sunday."[69]

More than seventy years after it began publication, *The Call to Worship* continues to be an important tool for communication, teaching, and reflection on faith and its interaction with daily events.

Any Other Business?

That is typically the last question before a meeting is adjourned, and at Wyatt Park that means adjourned with prayer. This chapter on organization concludes with an acknowledgment and a reminder. Acknowledged is the truth that the way Wyatt Park Christian Church organizes itself in the future will, and

---

68 *The Call to Worship*, April 28, 1999.
69 *The Call to Worship*, September 12, 2001.

indeed should, change as circumstances change. The reminder harkens back to the words with which this chapter began. If Wyatt Park Christian Church is to thrive in the twenty-first century, it must heed the words of Paul: "And he (Christ) is the head of the body, the church. He is the beginning, the firstborn from the dead, that in everything he might be preeminent" (Col. 1:18).

CHAPTER 8

Shepherds of the Flock

———

And I heard the voice of the Lord saying "Whom
shall I send, and who will go for us?"
Then I said, "Here I am! Send me." (Isa. 6:8)

Jesus said to Simon Peter, "Simon, son of John, do you love me
more than these?" He said to him, "Yes, Lord, you know that
I love you." He said to him, "Feed my lambs." (John 21:15)

PROTESTANTS AFFIRM THE "PRIESTHOOD OF all believers," an idea that is based
on 1 Peter 2:9. Peter referred to all who have received God's gift of salvation
when he wrote, "You are a chosen race, a royal priesthood, a holy nation, a
people for his own possession, that you may proclaim the excellencies of him
who called you out of darkness into his marvelous light." By virtue of baptism,
all Christians are called to proclaim the good news of what God has done in
Jesus Christ, but it is also true that some are called to Christian ministry as a
vocation. For some of those who are called to serve in a local congregation, it
is a full-time vocation, but for others, ministry in a local church is part-time,
done by one who may be semi-retired or engaged in full-time employment
elsewhere. Whether full-time or part-time, those who are called to the vocation of ministry understand that they are answerable above all to God and
that their task is to work within the setting of a local congregation to fulfill
the Great Commission (Matt. 28:19–20), to make and grow disciples of Jesus
Christ.

In this chapter, those who have served Wyatt Park Christian Church as pastors are briefly profiled. They have done their work under a variety of titles: Pastor, Senior Pastor, Associate Pastor, Assistant Pastor, and so forth. Also listed are those who have served as Directors or Ministers of Christian Education and as Youth Directors or Youth Pastors. Finally, there is a listing of Wyatt Park's "Timothy's" and "Phoebe's," men and women who have gone forth from the congregation and into vocational ministry. Regardless of the title, the model for their work is Jesus himself, the Good Shepherd (John 10:11).

Early Pastors

With the exception of M. M. Goode (see chapter 1), who was instrumental in the founding of Wyatt Park Christian Church, little is known about the men who served as pastors in the congregation's earliest years. For the most part, only their names are known. Serving the church during its first eight years were L. H. Otto, Charles Stout, C. C. Ferguson, A. Reid, J. B. Lockhart, and W. A. Pruett. Will Woodson served the church for two years, beginning in 1896. He was also an elder of First Christian Church and was an enthusiastic supporter of that congregation's efforts to plant new churches throughout the city. Woodson Chapel Christian Church on St. Joseph Avenue is named for him.

After serving as the pastor at First Christian Church for seventeen years, M. M. Goode became the pastor at Wyatt Park in 1898 and continued in that capacity until 1911. He was followed during the next four years by J. T. Shreve, J. M. Asbell, W. S. Priest, and T. E. Tomberlin.[1] John Love became the pastor in 1915 and served until 1921. It was during his ministry that the first money was raised for the construction of a new church building. Rev. Love was succeeded by Rev. J. Arthur Dillinger, who served Wyatt Park for five years.

---

1 Information about the earliest pastors is found in a brief history of the congregation written during the ministry of Rev. Tommie Bouchard (1961–1966). A copy is found in the historical scrapbook, 1887–1948.

John Keplinger (Pastor)
1927–1933

Rev. John Keplinger began his ministry at Wyatt Park in April 1927 after serving as pastor at the Christian Church in Union Star, Missouri. During his seven-year ministry there, he guided the congregation through the construction of a new building and that experience served him well at Wyatt Park.[2]

It was during his ministry that the Wyatt Park congregation bought property at Twenty-Seventh and Mitchell and constructed the building that was dedicated in October 1928. One year later, the Great Depression began, and by 1932 the board was forced to reduce the pastor's salary by one-third. It approved a budget reducing his annual salary from $2,250 per year to $1,500.[3] Rev. Keplinger informed the board that he would not be able to support his family on that salary, and he left Wyatt Park in the early summer, 1933. The *Call to Worship* noted his death in Tennessee in May 1952.[4]

Julian Stuart (Pastor)
1933–1940

Rev. Julian Stuart was called as pastor in October 1933. The Great Depression was underway, so initially he was called "on a monthly basis."[5] He served as pastor until September 1940, and his relationship with the congregation continued for another two decades.

A native of Buchanan County, Rev. Stuart was born near Rushville. He spent his early years on a farm and then moved to Atchison, Kansas, where he graduated from high school. He served churches in Kansas and Missouri before coming to Wyatt Park. Meeting minutes reveal few details about his ministry, but he was fondly remembered for many years after he left Wyatt Park to serve a church

---

2 *St. Joseph News-Press*, October 7, 1928.
3 Board minutes, December 9, 1932.
4 *The Call to Worship*, May 29, 1952.
5 Board minutes, November 1933 (exact date not indicated).

in California. He eventually held a leadership position with the denomination and returned to Wyatt Park multiple times as a guest speaker. Prior to visits in 1956 and 1961, he was recalled in *The Call to Worship*:

> He is remembered as one who brought stability and courage to this congregation during the days of the Great Depression. He was beloved as pastor and respected as a preacher.[6]
>
> Julian Stuart was for seven years Minister of Wyatt Park Christian Church, and coached it through difficult "depression" years. Many of us believe he literally saved the Church through his wise and statesman-like leadership.[7]

Rev. Stuart and his wife lost their lives in an auto accident in 1979.[8]

JOSEPH HOUSTON (PASTOR)
1940–1943

Rev. Joseph Houston was called to be Wyatt Park's pastor in November 1940.[9] Available documents reveal little about what he did before coming to Wyatt Park, except that he was a "preacher who used to teach agriculture."[10] He had an evangelistic bent. During his ministry of just over two years, 114 people united with Wyatt Park, and if a 1941 letter is any indication, then he was willing to combine his two vocations to reach people outside the church. The letter, from November 1941, was sent to "the farmers and suburban dwellers who live in the districts most accessible to the church." He invited them to a special Harvest Home service the Sunday evening after Thanksgiving. Congregation members who worked in grain milling and at the St. Joseph

---

6 *The Call to Worship*, May 16, 1956.

7 *The Call to Worship*, March 9, 1961.

8 *The Call to Worship*, November 21, 1979.

9 Board minutes, November 10, 1940.

10 "Letter of Introduction," November 21, 1941, filed in historical scrapbook, 1887–1948.

Stockyards participated in the service and also served as hosts. In the letter, Rev. Houston noted a population trend that is even more evident today:

> Knowing that modern transportation has affected the community life of the farmer and that many of the country churches have either closed or do not have active programs, the Wyatt Park Christian Church is simply offering you the Christian fellowship of a church located near the edge of St. Joseph…If you are now an active member of some church, splendid! If you are not now enjoying a church home, we most cordially invite you to get acquainted with us this Sunday evening at 7:30.[11]

Joseph Houston left Wyatt Park in February 1943 to become pastor at First Christian Church in Independence, Missouri. He later served churches in Nebraska, Texas, and Iowa.

LAWRENCE BASH (PASTOR)
1943–1949

Regardless of how long a local church has existed, there are certain pastors who stand out, maybe because of when they were at the church, or because of something specific that was accomplished during their tenure, or both. At Wyatt

Park, the names of two pastors come up often and with fondness. One of them is Lawrence Bash, who served the congregation for six years, beginning in 1943.

His father was also a pastor, and the family moved around a bit as he grew up. He graduated from high school in Wichita Falls, Texas, and then spent two years doing mission work in South Africa. When he returned to the United States, he continued his education at Drake University and later at the University of Chicago.[12]

---

11 Ibid.
12 *The Kansas City Star*, Obituary, Dr. Lawrence Bash, July 24, 1999.

His first contact with Wyatt Park came in April 1942 when he was invited to preach at a series of evangelistic services just after Easter. At the time, he was serving the Christian Church in Auburn, Nebraska.[13] In early 1943, he was called to be the pastor at Wyatt Park and began what would be a very successful ministry.[14]

During his tenure, the church grew significantly in terms of worship attendance, baptisms, Sunday-School participation, and outreach (missions) support. It was also during his tenure that the need for additional Christian education space was recognized. A building fund was established, and that eventually led to the construction of an addition to the three-story section of the facility that is used today for Christian education, Parents' Day Out/Pre-School, and Jacob's Closet.

Dr. Bash left Wyatt Park in 1949 and served as the pastor of University Christian Church in Austin, Texas, for ten years. On New Year's Day, 1960, he became pastor of Country Club Christian Church in Kansas City and held that position until his retirement in 1978. He died at his home in Kansas City in 1999.

WILLIAM SCHLEIFFARTH (ASSISTANT PASTOR) 1946–1948

Ministry staffing at Wyatt Park took an important step forward in 1946 with the calling of William Schlieffarth as Assistant Pastor. According to available documents, this was the first time that Wyatt Park had more than one person on the pastoral staff. Rev. Schleiffarth was a St. Louis native and had served small churches while attending college and then seminary. At Wyatt Park, he was primarily responsible for youth programming and Christian education.[15] He left Wyatt Park in 1948 to serve three Atchison County, Missouri, churches: Rock Port, Tarkio, and Linden. It was noted that he "will preach at all three churches each Sunday, but will live in Tarkio at the parsonage."[16] From Tarkio,

---

13 Flier, "Evangelistic Services," April 1942, filed with worship bulletins, 1941–1942.

14 Board minutes, February 11, 1943.

15 Worship Bulletin, September 1, 1946.

16 *The Call to Worship*, September 2, 1948.

he moved to First Christian Church in Brookfield, Missouri, and eventually retired to Kimberling City, Missouri, in 1982. He died in 1996.[17]

MERWIN COAD (ASSISTANT PASTOR)
1948–1949

William Schleiffarth was succeeded as Assistant Pastor by Merwin Coad. He grew up in Nebraska but had lived in Texas for several years before coming to Wyatt Park. Mr. Coad studied at Texas Christian University and was a pastor in Graham, Texas. At Wyatt Park, he directed youth programming and Christian education.[18] As noted in chapter 3, he also hosted a daily devotional broadcast on KRES Radio (1230 AM). His tenure was brief. Several months after beginning his ministry, he resigned to serve a church in Lenox, Iowa. The location also allowed him to complete his education at Drake Bible College in Des Moines. His resignation was announced in the newsletter, just a few weeks after Rev. Lawrence Bash resigned: "We are sorry to lose Merwin. This is, however, in keeping with the usual procedure when a minister leaves. The new minister will be enabled to build his own staff."[19]

Merwin Coad's life turned in a new direction when he was elected to represent Iowa in the US Congress in 1956. He served two terms. Since then, he has been engaged in residential and commercial construction and currently lives in Washington, D.C.[20]

TOM TOLER (PASTOR)
1949–1959

As noted above, in local churches that have existed for many years, there are certain pastors who stand out. Lawrence Bash is one of those pastors at Wyatt Park. Tom Toler, who served the congregation for nearly ten years, is the other.

---

17 *Springfield News-Leader*, Obituary, Ann Burrows Schleiffarth, May 16, 2012.

18 *The Call to Worship*, September 2, 1948.

19 *The Call to Worship*, February 24, 1949.

20 www.bioguide.congress.gov/scripts/biodisplay.pl?index=C000540, accessed June 15, 2017.

Dr. Toler was born in Guthrie Center, Iowa, but grew up in Kansas City. After high school, he went to college in Tennessee and then Michigan. He earned his master's degree at Phillips University in Oklahoma and his doctorate at Culver-Stockton in Canton, Missouri.[21] Dr. Toler came to Wyatt Park after serving as minister of Christian education at Country Club Christian Church in Kansas City. He began his ministry here in April 1949, although that was not Wyatt Park's first exposure to him, as he had spoken at one of Wyatt Park's youth retreats in 1945.[22] During his  ministry, Dr. Toler led the church through the final year of one building program (the three-story Education Building) and through the planning, design, and construction of the sanctuary. It was also during his ministry that the church experienced its most significant numerical growth.

He was actively involved in the Christian Church (Disciples of Christ) and in 1958 was elected vice president of the National Evangelistic Association.[23] Denominational leadership was a family affair. In 1957, his wife, Erma, was elected secretary of the state Christian Women's Fellowship. That same year, their daughter, Nancy, was elected secretary of the state Christian Youth Fellowship.

Nancy Toler's election is especially significant because three years earlier, during the fall of 1954, the congregation had supported the Tolers as she struggled with polio. Nancy was hospitalized for two months at Methodist Hospital, finally going home in early December.[24]

Tom Toler submitted his resignation in December 1958, and in February 1959, he became the pastor at First Christian Church in Oakland, California. He served there for ten years and then served for another twelve years at First

---

21 *The Bakersfield Californian*, Obituary, Dr. Thomas Wilbert Toler, July 7, 2004.

22 Worship bulletin, September 9, 1945.

23 *St. Joseph News-Press*, October 18, 1958.

24 *The Call to Worship*, October 7, 1954, October 14, 1954, November 11, 1954, November 25, 1954, and December 2, 1954.

Christian Church in Bakersfield, California, from which he retired in 1979. Dr. Toler was still living in Bakersfield when he went home to the Lord in July 2004.[25]

CLAYTON POTTER (PASTOR)
1959–1961

Clayton Potter began his ministry at Wyatt Park in June 1959, but he was well known to the congregation for more than a decade before his call to St. Joseph. He was the pastor of South Street Christian Church in Springfield, Missouri, when he visited Wyatt Park as the featured speaker during a week-long Visitation Evangelism Campaign in 1946.[26] He served as guest speaker again in 1957 when the 118th State Convention of Christian Churches in Missouri was held in St. Joseph.[27] Rev. Potter was serving a church in Shreveport, Louisiana, when he was called to Wyatt Park.

His résumé was impressive with especially successful pastorates in Springfield. Most notable was his leadership of the newly formed National Avenue Christian Church, which grew to more than eight hundred members during his nine-year tenure.[28] A 1959 pastor's column provides a peek into his ministry. He essentially shared his *log* for the week, and it included visits to numerous church members in the hospital or at their homes, appearances at King Hill Christian Church and First Christian Church in Maryville, multiple meetings, attendance at church dinners and a Wednesday Bazaar, and "Long evenings in the study, frequently exchanging ideas with Bill Hutchings" (Associate Pastor).[29]

Rev. Potter's tenure at Wyatt Park was brief, less than two years. He resigned in February 1961 to become Associate Executive Director of the

---

25 *The Bakersfield Californian*, Obituary, Dr. Thomas Wilbert Toler, July 7, 2004.

26 *The Call to Worship*, October 17, 1946.

27 *The Call to Worship*, May 1, 1957.

28 Pulpit Committee report, filed with board minutes, February 9, 1959.

29 *The Call to Worship*, December 10, 1959.

Texas Christian Churches.[30] He returned to ministry in the local church a few years later and was serving as pastor of Ridglea Christian Church in Fort Worth when he died in 1971 following a heart attack.

WILLIAM "BILL" HUTCHINGS (ASSOCIATE PASTOR) 1959–1962

At different times since the mid-twentieth century, Wyatt Park Christian Church has called people to serve as Minister (or Director) of Christian Education, and they are briefly profiled in the Ministers of Education section below. There have also been men and women called to the role of Associate (or Assistant) Pastor, whose responsibilities were more wide-ranging but often included Christian education. Such was the case with William "Bill" Hutchings, who was called as Associate Pastor in 1959.

A native of St. Louis, Rev. Hutchings was twenty-seven years old when he came to Wyatt Park. He graduated from the University of Missouri and then the College of the Bible (now Lexington Theological Seminary) in Lexington, Kentucky, and was serving the Christian Church in Tarkio, Missouri, when he was called to Wyatt Park. His responsibilities at Wyatt Park included Christian education, youth work, membership development, and leadership recruitment and training. A reminder to the congregation at the time of his calling is worth noting at any time:

> This must be emphasized: If Mr. Hutchings does the work for which he has been called, we will be needing FAR MORE, not less, lay workers in an expanding program of Christian life within our congregation.[31]

During his tenure, Christian education and youth ministries were reorganized with new, trained leaders put in place, and new classes added. Rev. Hutchings

---

30 *The Call to Worship*, February 23, 1961.
31 *The Call to Worship*, November 19, 1959.

left Wyatt Park in March 1962 to join the ministry staff of Central Christian Church in Dallas, Texas.[32]

TOMMIE BOUCHARD (PASTOR)
1961–1966

Wyatt Park's ministry connection with Texas continued with the calling of Rev. Tommie Bouchard as pastor in August 1961. The Texas native was serving First Christian Church in Mineral Wells, Texas, when he was called to St. Joseph. He was a graduate of Texas Christian University and served as Youth Director for the Texas Board of Christian Churches before beginning his ministry at Mineral Wells.[33]

In his first report to the church board, Rev. Bouchard shared his weekly schedule and noted that it "includes a proposed afternoon of rest on Wednesday and Saturday. Perhaps at a later date it will be possible to set aside a full day for rest."[34] Whether his schedule ever changed to include a full day off is unknown, but there was certainly plenty to keep him busy. The environment in which he did his ministry might best be described as "turbulent," not at Wyatt Park, but culturally and within the denomination.

Culturally, the Civil Rights Movement was emerging with an increase in organized marches, acts of civil disobedience, and race riots in many cities. As America's involvement in the Vietnam War escalated, so did protests against it. Antiwar sentiment was widespread and was especially evident on college campuses where sit-ins and other forms of protest became commonplace. As noted in the previous chapter, Rev. Bouchard often wrote and spoke about the changing culture and how it intersected with the gospel of Jesus Christ (see chapter 7).

The 1960s was also a time of challenging transition within the Christian Church (Disciples of Christ) as the denomination formally restructured itself

---

32 *The Call to Worship*, March 1, 1962, and March 8, 1962.
33 *The Call to Worship*, August 10, 1961.
34 Minister's report, September 11, 1961.

in 1968, a move that prompted more than three thousand congregations to withdraw (see chapter 7). Rev. Bouchard was among 120 people who served on the Commission on Restructure, the body that met and worked for several years to develop the plan of denominational restructure.

The Lone Star State's tug on the heart of the Texas native was strong, and in 1966, he resigned to accept a call to become the pastor of First Christian Church in Longview, Texas.[35] Tommie Bouchard was still living in Texas at the time of his death in August 1980.

LOYAL NORTHCOTT (PASTOR) 1967–1968

In what became a pattern, at least for a few years, the Texas connection continued with the calling of Rev. Loyal Northcott to be Wyatt Park's pastor. The Kansas native served First Christian Church in Tyler, Texas, for nine years before coming to St. Joseph. He had also served churches in Atchison, Kansas, and Ponca City, Oklahoma. Additionally, he held several national leadership positions within the Christian Church (Disciples of Christ).

His ministry at Wyatt Park began in January 1967. A few months after his arrival, construction began on the addition that was dedicated in 1968, and as often happens with such a project, it disrupted life around the church. Rev. Northcott noted the disruption in his December report to the board:

> The noise of construction has not been so great this month but the disruptiveness of [our] program has gone on. We have several more months of rebuilding and renovation and then we can rejoice in the new opportunities.[36]

---

35 *The Call to Worship*, August 25, 1966.
36 Minister's report, December 1, 1967.

In that same report, he spoke about the need to solve two ongoing problems:

> I would like to invite the Board Members to help me in this closing month of 1967 to pray for God's help and understanding our failures and what we can do to "break through" on the matter of church attendance and evangelism.[37]

Rev. Northcott's commitment to the important role of evangelism in church life contributed to an announcement a few months later that surprised both him and the congregation. On June 30, 1968, less than eighteen months after beginning his ministry at Wyatt Park, Loyal Northcott resigned. He accepted the call to a denominational position as Executive Secretary of the Department of Evangelism and Membership. Such a turn of events had not been anticipated, but he concluded that the call was one he could not refuse. The closing sentence of his resignation letter is a timeless reminder for all who care about ministry in the local church: "The days ahead for your congregation and the whole church demand no less than the first century demanded of the church in that day."[38] His observation is even more relevant today.

After his retirement, Rev. Northcott returned to Tyler, Texas, and to membership in the congregation where he had formerly served as pastor at First Christian Church. He died in January 1997.[39]

RICHARD TARR (ASSOCIATE PASTOR) 1967–1969

In September 1967, the congregation again looked to Texas for ministry staff. Rev. Richard Tarr was called as Associate Pastor, coming to Wyatt Park after serving as pastor of First Christian Church in Sweetwater, Texas. The West Virginia native graduated from Texas Christian University and its affiliated

---

37 Ibid.

38 *The Call to Worship*, July 11, 1968.

39 Harvey County Genealogical Database, accessed July 17, 2017, http://www.hcgsks.org/harcodatabase/showmedia.php?&mediaID=48806&page=3509.

Brite Divinity School. In addition to the congregation at Sweetwater, he served four other congregations in Texas and Kansas before coming to Wyatt Park.[40] Christian education was a primary area of responsibility at Wyatt Park, but after Rev. Loyal Northcott resigned in June 1968, Rev. Tarr's responsibilities increased. His ministry at Wyatt Park lasted almost exactly two years. He resigned in September 1969 to return to Texas as pastor of the Christian Church in Levelland, west of Lubbock.[41]

WILLIAM "BILL" MALOTTE (PASTOR) 1969–1976

William Malotte became Wyatt Park's pastor in September 1970. The Oklahoma native studied at Phillips University and Vanderbilt University and was serving as Vice-President for Development at the Missouri School of Religion in Columbia when he was called to Wyatt Park. He had also served churches in Arkansas, Tennessee, and Oklahoma.[42]

Three months after his arrival, Rev. Malotte introduced the New Generation Singers (see chapter 3) for their first performance. It was in December 1970, and he concluded his introduction with the words "Let the music begin." Forty years later, in 2010, New-G presented a fortieth anniversary performance at Wyatt Park, and William Malotte was in attendance, having traveled from his home in Springfield, Missouri. Again he introduced the group, with the words "Let the music begin."

Unlike most pastors, Rev. Malotte was willing to be political, at least a bit. He used his newsletter pastor's column to encourage voter support of a school bond issue in 1971, and later that year he used the same forum to urge a vote against the proposed legalization of pari-mutuel betting in Missouri.[43] He continued the anti-gambling theme in 1974 in response to a proposed constitutional amendment to legalize gambling in Missouri:

---

40 Board minutes, September 11, 1967, and *The Call to Worship*, September 28, 1967.
41 *The Call to Worship*, September 18, 1969.
42 Board minutes, July 21, 1969, and *The Call to Worship*, August 7, 1969.
43 *The Call to Worship*, January 28, 1971, and September 23, 1971.

Should this vote come in 1974, and it likely will, I hope every member of this congregation will vote against it for moral reasons. There are no redeeming qualities in gambling…Gambling breeds crime, corruption, and hurts legitimate business. It is also a poor source of revenue, but what is really wrong with gambling is that it hurts people. Let's not change our constitution to aid vice-merchants and destroy many Missourians.[44]

Rev. Malotte resigned his position at Wyatt Park in May 1976 to become the District Minister for District Nine (Springfield) of the Christian Church in Missouri.[45] He was still living in Springfield when he retired from ministry. He currently lives in Surprise, Arizona.

DARRELL BIGGS (ASSOCIATE PASTOR) 1970–1972

A native of the northwest Kansas town of St. Francis, Rev. Darrell Biggs, was called to be Associate Pastor in April 1970. He came to Wyatt Park from Dallas, Texas, where he was the Minister of Education in a Disciples of Christ congregation. In addition, he served as chairman of Christian education for the Dallas Area Association of Christian Churches. He was called to Wyatt Park to oversee Christian education and membership activities.[46] There was plenty to do because Sunday-School attendance averaged between 250 and 300 during those years. A little more than two years after he began his ministry at Wyatt Park, he resigned to accept a ministry position in Austin, Minnesota.[47] His final years in ministry were spent in the southeast Kansas town of Girard. He lives in Temple, Texas.

---

44 *The Call to Worship*, March 14, 1974.
45 *The Call to Worship*, May 6, 1976.
46 *The Call to Worship*, April 16, 1970.
47 *The Call to Worship*, August 31, 1972.

BYRON MYERS (ASSOCIATE PASTOR, ETC.)
1959–1980

Byron Myers wore multiple hats during his lengthy tenure at Wyatt Park. His work was primarily in the areas of music and youth, but for a few years, he also had the title of Associate Pastor. The St. Joseph native first came to Wyatt Park in 1959 as Director of the Chancel and Sanctuary Choirs, and he served in that capacity for several years. At the time he came to Wyatt Park, he was also employed as choral director at his alma mater, Central High School.[48]

In 1972, he joined the Wyatt Park staff full-time with the title of Director of Music and Youth Activities. In addition to oversight of all church activities pertaining to music and youth, he was called to "assist the minister in giving general leadership to the total church program."[49] By 1976, his title was Minister of Music and Youth and at some point, although the documents are unclear as to when, his title became Associate Pastor. He was approved for ordination by the Christian Church of Missouri in June 1977 and was ordained during morning worship the following September.[50]

Citing multiple reasons, the board decided in January 1979 to return his position to part-time with the title, Director/Manager of New Generation Singers.[51] One year later, the board approved a Personnel Committee recommendation that the position become nonpaid, with the Director/Manager of the New Generation Singers serving as a volunteer.[52] As a result Byron Myers left Wyatt Park, along with the New Generation Singers and several church members who followed New-G to its new home at Ashland United Methodist Church. It took several years for the wound of New-G's departure to heal at Wyatt Park. The group continues to rehearse at Ashland UMC.

---

48 *The Call to Worship*, September 3, 1959.

49 *The Call to Worship*, September 21, 1972.

50 *The Call to Worship*, June 16, 1977, and September 15, 1977.

51 Board minutes, January 8, 1979, and January 28, 1979.

52 Board minutes, December 13, 1979, and January 27, 1980.

L. WALLACE "WALLY" BROWN (PASTOR) 1976–1987

Lynn Wallace "Wally" Brown was called to serve as Wyatt Park's pastor in October 1976. He was born in Ohio but grew up in Kansas City. Rev. Brown graduated from Texas Christian University and Brite Divinity School, both located in Fort Worth. Prior to his ministry at Wyatt Park, he served churches in Texas and Missouri.[53]

Significant challenges plagued his tenure, as it was during his ministry that the New Generation Singers left the church, taking many congregation members with them. Their departure left a deep wound and ill feelings that lingered for several years. Nationwide, the children of baby boomers were beginning to leave churches in large numbers, as America's transition to a more secular culture got underway. A 1987 minister's report to the board is illustrative of the difficult times. Consisting mostly of thoughts and phrases, rather than complete sentences, Rev. Brown responded to his critics by defending his own record and by taking the congregation to task for "dragging their feet" and so on. He noted several positive developments, including growth in children's ministries, expanded staff, taking initial steps toward construction of what would become Danford Hall, the return to a Sunday morning schedule including two worship services, and significant updating of office equipment.[54] He resigned in October 1987 and served congregations in Cape Girardeau and Warrensburg, Missouri, before retiring in 2000. Wally Brown lived in Georgetown, Texas, at the time of his death, on May 4, 2016.[55]

RALPH SAWYER (MINISTER OF PASTORAL CARE) 1979–1987

Ralph Sawyer served in so many ways through the years that he may be the most difficult person of all to place under a single heading. As noted in other

---

53 Board minutes, September 30, 1976, and *WPCC Program*, 1983 booklet filed in historical scrapbook, 1978–1987.

54 Minister's report filed with board minutes, March 23, 1987.

55 *The Kansas City Star*, Obituaries, May 12, 2016.

chapters, he was an elder, a teacher, and chairman of the board for many years. Both of his sons were ordained pastors. Mr. Sawyer became a licensed minister within the Christian Church (Disciples of Christ) and for several years served as pastor of the rural Bethany Christian Church, in Clinton County, Missouri, where he preached twice each month. He was also often called upon by area funeral homes to conduct services for people who did not have a pastor.

In 1979, he became a part of the ministry staff at Wyatt Park and went on to serve for eight years as Minister of Pastoral Care. In that role, he visited people in the hospital and in their homes, assisted with pastoral care work at the church, and conducted funerals when the Senior Pastor was unavailable. He concluded his tenure on the church staff December 31, 1987. He died in January 1993.

William "Bill" McCutchen (Associate Pastor) 1980–1984

William "Bill" McCutchen was called to the position of Associate Pastor in January 1980. He came to Wyatt Park from a similar position in Manhattan, Kansas. Rev. McCutchen graduated from Phillips University and then Phillips Seminary in Enid, Oklahoma. When he arrived at Wyatt Park, he was pursuing a doctorate through San Francisco Theological Seminary.[56] He came with extensive training in youth work and family counseling. As Associate Pastor, he was involved in all areas of the congregation's programming and ministries.

Rev. McCutchen resigned on June 11, 1984, to become Associate Regional Minister for the Christian Church (Disciples of Christ) in Florida. Several years ago, he returned to his home state of Oklahoma and has since focused his attention on ministry to the Native American population and studying Native American spirituality.[57]

---

56 Board minutes, January 20, 1980.
57 https://www.facebook.com/mccutchen.bill, accessed July 3, 2017.

GREG AND KAREN GUY (CO-ASSOCIATE PASTORS) 1985–1988

Wyatt Park Christian Church took an unusual, but not unheard of, step in 1985 when it called a married couple to the position of Co-Associate Pastors. Greg and Karen Guy came to Wyatt Park after completing Master of Divinity degrees at Lexington Theological Seminary in Lexington, Kentucky.[58]

At the time they were called, there were approximately 120 clergy couples serving in the Christian Church (Disciples of Christ), but very few shared the role of Associate Pastor. At Wyatt Park, the Guys had different areas of responsibility. Greg Guy focused on membership development, while Karen Guy focused on Christian education and children's programming.[59]

They resigned in August 1988 after Rev. Greg Guy was called to be the Senior Pastor of First Christian Church in Santa Barbara, California.[60] In the years that followed, the couple returned to the Midwest and, sadly, eventually divorced. Greg Guy continued in ministry and most recently served as pastor of First Christian Church in Owenton, Kentucky.[61] Karen Lorack Mitchell works as a preschool teacher in Littleton, Colorado.[62]

M. EUGENE "GENE" MOCKABEE (PASTOR) 1989–2005

Dr. M. Eugene "Gene" Mockabee began his ministry at Wyatt Park in January 1989, the start of what would be the longest tenured senior pastorate in the congregation's history. A native of Concordia, Kansas, he had served congregations in Kalispell, Montana, and Plattsmouth, Nebraska, before coming to Wyatt Park. His undergraduate degree (Kansas State University) was in

---

58 Board minutes, May 6, 1985.

59 *St. Joseph News-Press*, 1986 (exact date not available). Filed in historical scrapbook, 1978–1986.

60 *The Call to Worship*, July 21, 1988.

61 *Yearbook & Directory*, Christian Church (Disciples of Christ), 2016.

62 https://www.facebook.com/karen.lorackmitchell?fref=search, accessed July 5, 2017.

electrical engineering, and he earned both his Master of Divinity and Doctor of Ministry degrees at Lexington Theological Seminary in Kentucky.[63]

His seventeen-year ministry at Wyatt Park enabled the congregation to heal the still-open wound that stemmed from the departure of the New Generation Singers in 1980. Significant mile-stones were reached during his tenure, including the completion and dedication of Danford Hall (1990); the addition of the Social Hall, offices, Atrium, and basement fellowship areas, along with renovation of the Mitchell Avenue entrance (1994); the addition of contemporary-praise-style worship (1997); and the addition of a Saturday-evening contemporary-praise-style worship service (2001). He learned HTML (hypertext markup language) and created Wyatt Park's first web page at a time when few other local congregations yet had a presence on the Internet. In the days before his retirement at the end of 2005, he reminisced in the newsletter about the all-important ministry of pastoral care:

> In going through books and records and files, what memories! Mostly good and joy-filled memories, but some sad ones, too. After all, we shared an awful lot. I mentioned the names Sunday of some of those not present that I sure miss. There have been a lot of tears with you over those wonderful people now gone. But there have been even more smiles and laughs.[64]

Dr. Mockabee stayed in St. Joseph for a while after retiring but now lives in New Hampshire.

---

63 *The Call to Worship*, January 12, 1989.
64 *The Call to Worship*, December 28, 2005.

SCOTT KILLGORE (ASSOCIATE PASTOR/SENIOR PASTOR) 1996–

In February 1996, the church board and congregation extended a call to me to become the Associate Pastor of Wyatt Park Christian Church. I had just completed seminary education in Kentucky and prior to that had spent seventeen years in broadcast journalism. As a native of the area, coming home to northwest Missouri offered the potential for a good "fit" and productive ministry. In the position to which I was called, I would be a pastor to the entire congregation but with emphasis on youth and young families.[65] Those areas of emphasis were lived out in multiple ways, and they came together in February 1997 when the congregation first offered contemporary-praise-style worship (see chapter 3).

Dr. Mockabee announced to the congregation in February 2005 that he intended to retire as Senior Pastor at the end of that year.[66] A search team was formed, and after several meetings it recommended that I be called to succeed Dr. Mockabee as Senior Pastor upon his retirement. For an Associate Pastor to succeed a Senior Pastor was not unheard of in the Christian Church (Disciples of Christ), but it was unusual. Nevertheless, the church board agreed with the search team's recommendation, as did the congregation a few weeks later.[67] The timing of the decision coincided with my completion of a Doctor of Ministry at Fuller Theological Seminary. My work as the Senior Pastor of Wyatt Park Christian Church began on January 1, 2006, and continues today.

CHAD MATTINGLY (ASSOCIATE PASTOR) 2006–2007

Rev. Chad Mattingly began his ministry at Wyatt Park in January 2006, and his calling marked the first time that the congregation employed a full-time minister from *outside* the Christian Church (Disciples of Christ). Rev.

---

65 Board minutes, January 29, 1996, and *The Call to Worship*, February 22, 1996.

66 "Letter to the Elders" dated January 3, 2005, filed with board minutes, and *The Call to Worship*, February 2, 2005.

67 Board minutes, April 18, 2005, and *The Call to Worship*, May 25, 2005.

Mattingly was ordained in the American Baptist Church and came to Wyatt Park from First Baptist Church in Gaithersburg, Maryland.[68]

Changing times made that step both necessary and possible. It was necessary because the number of qualified candidates from within the Disciples of Christ had become very small, especially for positions other than Senior Pastor. It was possible because of Internet staff recruiting resources that were not available even a few years earlier. The decision to look outside the Disciples of Christ was both illustrative of, and the result of, a trend across North America—the diminishing role of traditional denominations.

At Wyatt Park, Rev. Mattingly was a pastor to the entire congregation, with emphasis on adult spiritual growth: Sunday School, small group development, Bible study and prayer groups, and Christian service ministries. He also taught (preached) regularly in worship, but with the retirement of Gene Mockabee, it was no longer the practice to have both pastors teach every weekend. Instead, one pastor would teach in all weekend services, and Rev. Mattingly taught approximately one weekend per month.

Within a year of their arrival at Wyatt Park, the Mattinglys learned that their young son had autism, and they made the decision to move to Springfield, Missouri, where he could enroll in a school that works exclusively with autistic children.[69] Rev. Mattingly left Wyatt Park in May 2007 after being called to become the Associate Pastor at Nixa Christian Church, just south of Springfield. He eventually became the Senior Pastor there and now serves as the Senior Pastor at Kingwood Christian Church in Kingwood, Texas, a suburb of Houston.

MIKE CAMPBELL (ASSOCIATE PASTOR)
2007–2011

In the summer of 2007, the board and congregation voted to call a Pennsylvania native, Mike Campbell, to be Wyatt Park's next Associate Pastor. He

---

68 *The Call to Worship*, November 9, 2005.
69 *The Call to Worship*, May 1, 2007.

was fifty years old and had spent over twenty-five years in secular employment before surrendering to the call to ministry and attending seminary. His responsibilities at Wyatt Park were similar to those of his predecessor, Chad Mattingly—namely, be a pastor to the entire congregation but focus especially on adult spiritual growth. As was the case with the calling of Rev. Mattingly, the decision to call Mike Campbell marked a change in how the congregation recruits ministry staff.

Although Pastor Campbell had a master's degree from Dallas Theological Seminary, he was not ordained, making him the first person called to the position of pastor at Wyatt Park who did not have that credential. He did become licensed by the Christian Church (Disciples of Christ), a credential that is similar to ordination but with some limitations.[70]

During his tenure at Wyatt Park, he discerned gifts for ministry to hospital patients, and in 2011, he resigned to become a chaplain resident at Baptist Medical Center in Jacksonville, Florida.[71] The move enabled him to further explore hospital ministry, and to return to Jacksonville, where he and his family had lived when he left secular employment to attend seminary. Mr. Campbell still lives in the Jacksonville area.

Jessica Schwartz Stan (Pastor to Children and Youth/Associate Pastor)
2007–2012

Jessica Schwartz was called to be Director of Children's and Youth Ministries in April 2007. She came to Wyatt Park from her home state of Maryland, where she had grown up in the United Methodist Church. She had earned a bachelor's degree in music with additional emphasis on youth ministry, which served her well as she oversaw ministry to Wyatt Park children and youth.[72] She also assisted in other areas of ministry and regularly taught during weekend worship. In time, her title was changed to Pastor to Children and Youth,

---

70 *The Call to Worship*, July 17, 2007.

71 *The Call to Worship*, February 15, 2011.

72 Cabinet minutes, April 16, 2007, and *The Call to Worship*, April 17, 2007.

and, in time, her name was changed to Jessica Stan. She and Kevin Stan were married in July 2008 at Wyatt Park.

Mike Campbell's departure in 2011 left vacant the position of Associate Pastor, and in July 2011, the congregation called Ms. Stan to that position.[73] The position was realigned to include youth ministry, and she remained as Associate Pastor until October 2012 when family circumstances necessitated a move to Seattle. She currently lives in suburban Seattle and is involved in both prayer ministry and music ministry at her church.

STEFFANIE BISHOP (CHILDREN'S PASTOR/FAMILY PASTOR) 2012–2015

Following the decision to call Jessica Stan to the position of Associate Pastor, the search began for a Children's Pastor. It concluded with the calling of Steffanie Bishop, who joined the Wyatt Park ministry staff in January 2012. She grew up Roman Catholic but had been in the Southern Baptist Church before coming to Wyatt Park. Ms. Bishop had spent several years in secular employment before surrendering to the call to ministry. Her education included a Master's Degree in Religious Education from Liberty University. Prior to the family's move to St. Joseph, she worked as an Associate Children's Minister at a large Southern Baptist Church in suburban San Antonio, Texas, where she also taught at a Christian school.[74]

Her duties expanded in early 2014 as she assumed oversight of youth ministry and some ministry to young families. The expansion of responsibilities was accompanied by an expanded title, Family Pastor. By early 2015, she concluded that her calling was in the elementary classroom, and she resigned to complete work on Missouri teacher certification.[75] She currently teaches at St. Joseph Christian School.

---

73 *The Call to Worship*, July 5, 2011, and July 19, 2011.

74 *The Call to Worship*, November 1, 2011, and December 6, 2011.

75 *The Call to Worship*, January 22, 2013.

Scott McNay (Associate Pastor)
2013

A Kansas City native, Scott McNay, was called to be Associate Pastor in January 2013, and he began his ministry at Wyatt Park several weeks later. His background was in the independent Christian Church, another denomination rooted in the same Campbell-Stone reform movement from which the Disciples of Christ began. He earned a Bachelor's Degree in Ministry from Central Christian College of the Bible, and he spent nine years as a local church pastor before coming to Wyatt Park.[76] As Associate Pastor, he served the entire congregation, with emphasis on youth and young families. By year-end, he felt called to return to a smaller church and left to become the pastor at La Plata Christian Church near Kirksville, Missouri, where he still serves today.

Jeb Flynn (Associate Pastor)
2015—

Rev. Jeb Flynn became Associate Pastor in June 2015. As with his predecessors, he was called to be a pastor to the entire congregation but with emphasis on youth and young adults. He grew up in a non-denominational church in Abilene, Kansas. Rev. Flynn earned his bachelor's degree from Mid-America Nazarene University and then a Master's Degree in Theological Studies at Nazarene Theological Seminary. He was ordained by the Church of the Nazarene. Before coming to Wyatt Park, he did campus ministry at Johnson County Community College in Overland Park, Kansas.[77]

Today, he oversees ministry to youth and young adults, and he regularly teaches during worship. Additionally, he is helping the congregation grow in evangelism and in its efforts to bridge cultural divides as the gospel is proclaimed, something of increasing importance as St. Joseph becomes more multicultural.

---

76 *The Call to Worship*, January 22, 2013.
77 *The Call to Worship*, May 13, 2015.

MINISTERS (DIRECTORS) OF CHRISTIAN EDUCATION

Beginning in 1949 and continuing for most years through 2005, Wyatt Park Christian Church employed a staff member to oversee Christian education for all ages. Most were employed full-time, and many of them had at least some seminary training in the field of Christian education. The first Director of Religious Education was *Hazel Gates*, who began her work in June 1949. She left the church one year later.[78] She was succeeded by *Willa Mae Ray*, who served as Christian Education Director for three years, from October 1951 until November 1954, when she left to accept a similar position in Oklahoma City.[79] *Bill Herod* was called to be Minister of Christian Education in December 1954. He came to Wyatt Park after serving as pastor of First Christian Church in Brookfield, Missouri. As a part of Wyatt Park's mission to support congregations in outlying communities, Rev. Herod also served as the preacher two weekends each month at Agency Christian Church and two weekends each month at Faucett Christian Church. Rev. Herod left Wyatt Park in June 1956 to join the staff of First Christian Church in Oklahoma City.[80] During the late 1950s, Christian education was directed by Associate Pastor William Hutchings.

The next Minister of Christian Education, *Nelson Irving*, was called in May 1962. A native of Tulsa, Oklahoma, he graduated from Phillips University in Enid, Oklahoma, just before his arrival at Wyatt Park. One year later, his title was changed to Associate Pastor. His duties remained the same as before, but the title change was made "to add dignity to his name." He remained at Wyatt Park until January 1965, when he resigned to accept a call as pastor of Bellevue Christian Church near Omaha.[81] He was succeeded by *J. Cy Rowell*, who was called to be Minister of Christian Education in April 1965. He came to Wyatt Park after completing a Doctor of Theology

78 *The Call to Worship*, June 16, 1949, and June 1, 1950.

79 *The Call to Worship*, September 13, 1951, and Board Minutes, November 8, 1954.

80 Board minutes, December 13, 1954, and July 30, 1956, and *The Call to Worship*, January 6, 1955, and March 17, 1955.

81 Board minutes, May 14, 1962, and May 12, 1963, and *The Call to Worship*, January 21, 1965.

at Princeton Theological Seminary. He had also served as the Director of Leadership Education for the Christian Churches in Kentucky. Not quite two years after his arrival at Wyatt Park, he resigned to accept a teaching position at Drake University in Des Moines.[82] With the exception of two "interim" directors, there was not another Christian Education Director at Wyatt Park until October 1989 when *Carol St. Myers* was called to the position. She had a United Methodist background and served as Christian Education Director at Wyatt Park for eight years, until her resignation in April 1997. She accepted a similar position in a United Methodist congregation in St. Joseph.[83] After graduating from Phillips Theological Seminary, *Rev. Tammy Kanatzar*, became Director of Christian Education in August 1997. Following ordination, her title was changed to Minister of Christian Education. In addition to guiding Christian education, she did extensive ministry with hospital patients and shut-ins, and that work moved her ministry in a new direction. She resigned in April 2002 to enter a one-year chaplain residency at M.D. Anderson Hospital in Houston.[84] Today she serves as a hospital chaplain in Jefferson City, Missouri.

Rev. Kanatzar was the last person to hold a full-time Christian education position at Wyatt Park. She was succeeded by two part-time Christian Education Directors, *Orville Stacey* (2002–2003) and *Jeanette Mausolf* (2004–2005). Since 2005, responsibilities for oversight of Christian education have been handled by other ministry staff members.

MINISTRY TO CHILDREN AND YOUTH

Most of the time, ministry to children has been guided by Ministers (Directors) of Christian Education, and ministry to older youth has been guided by Associate Pastors. However, there have been times when someone was employed specifically for one of those tasks, usually on a part-time basis. The first was *Mae Louise Brown*, who began her work in September

---

82 *The Call to Worship*, July 1, 1965, and Board Minutes, August 1, 1967.

83 *The Call to Worship*, October 26, 1989, and April 21, 1997.

84 *The Call to Worship*, August 28, 1997, and April 17, 2002.

1944 as Director of Youth Activities.[85] How long she served in that staff position is unknown. *Craig Ritchie* was called as Youth Minister (part-time) in January 1990 and continued in that capacity for two years.[86] He was succeeded by *Mark View*, who was Youth Director for eighteen months, concluding in November 1994.[87] *Geoff Heckman* served as Youth Director for several months beginning in September 2000.[88] The position of Youth Director was made full-time in August 2001, and it was filled by *Sarah Canaday Heckman*. She continued in that ministry capacity until September 2005, when her family moved to Kansas City.[89] The current Director of Children's Ministries, *Tonya Ball*, joined the Wyatt Park ministry staff in May 2014.

Timothy's and Phoebe's

Men and women who engage in ministry as a vocation must come from *somewhere*, and for almost all of them, that *somewhere* is a local church. When a local church sends a man out into vocational ministry, he is referred to as a "Timothy" of the congregation, so named because of the young man (Timothy) sent out by the apostle Paul (Phil. 2:20–22; 1 Tim.; 2 Tim.). When a local church sends a woman out into vocational ministry, she is referred to as a "Phoebe" of the congregation, so named because of a woman commended by Paul for her significant role in the formation of the early church (Rom. 16:1–2). Wyatt Park Christian Church has sent many men and women into vocational ministry. Sadly, information about some of them is sparse.

The first person ordained to Christian ministry at Wyatt Park was *Rev. George L. Peters*. He was ordained on February 14, 1892, in the congregation's original building at Twenty-Seventh and Olive Streets. Following his

---

85 Worship bulletin, September 3, 1944.

86 *The Call to Worship*, January 4, 1990, and December 24, 1992.

87 *The Call to Worship*, April 1, 1993, and November 25, 1994.

88 *The Call to Worship*, September 20, 2000.

89 *The Call to Worship*, August 1, 2001, and board minutes, October 17, 2005.

ordination, he served as pastor of Maysville Christian Church and continued in ministry serving congregations in Missouri and surrounding states. He returned to Wyatt Park as guest speaker when the congregation celebrated its fiftieth anniversary in the summer of 1938.[90]

It was almost six decades before Wyatt Park sent out another man or woman into vocational ministry. *George "Billy" Barger* was ordained July 16, 1950. He visited Wyatt Park a few times while a ministerial student. Prior to his 1948 visit, the congregation was encouraged to show its support: "As the only minister sent out in sixty years by Wyatt Park Church, Billy has a special place in our interests and affection. Let us support him with great audiences next Sunday!"[91]

Next to be sent out from Wyatt Park were four women, but for the most part, all that is known about them are their names and the years that they were licensed or ordained: *Mae Louise Brown*, who directed Christian education at churches in North Carolina (1949); *Charlene Stewart* (1949); *Margaret Omdahl McKeown* (1950); and *Lois Stover Scott* (1953).

Galen Clark was ordained in March 1958 after graduating from the School of Religion at Drury College in Springfield, Missouri. *Carolee Recklefs Curtright* was sent into vocational ministry in 1956, and the name of *Mary Lou Stover Campbell* was added to the list of Phoebe's in 1961.

Rev. Kyle Maxwell graduated from the Divinity School at Phillips University and then the Harvard Divinity School. He was ordained at Wyatt Park Christian Church on July 30, 1961.[92] He spent thirty-four years as pastor of First Christian Church in Edmond, Oklahoma, a suburb of Oklahoma City. Since 2002, he has served on the staff of the Oklahoma Disciples Foundation.[93]

In May 1963, *Rev. Denton Roberts* was ordained to Christian ministry at Wyatt Park. He earned a Bachelor of Divinity from Drake University in Des

---

90 *St. Joseph News-Press*, summer 1938 (exact date unavailable), filed in historical scrapbook, 1887–1948.

91 *The Call to Worship*, June 17, 1948.

92 *The Call to Worship*, June 29, 1961, and July 27, 1961.

93 *The Edmond Sun*, November 4, 2005, and the Oklahoma Disciples Foundation, accessed July 16, 2017, http://okdfdn.org/.

Moines, Iowa, and, at the time of his ordination, served as pastor of Early Chapel Church in Earlham, Iowa.[94] *James Ream* received ministry credentials in 1965, and *Linda Pollard Bryant* received her credentials in 1969.

Rev. Randall Sawyer was ordained at Wyatt Park in September 1968. His ordination followed graduation from Texas Christian University and the Brite Divinity School.[95] His brother, *Rev. William Sawyer*, was ordained in 1971, also after graduating from Texas Christian University and the Brite Divinity School.[96] Randall and William Sawyer are the sons of Ralph and Juanita Sawyer (Ralph Sawyer is profiled above).

Rev. Kent Dannen graduated from Lexington (Kentucky) Theological Seminary in 1973 and was ordained the following February. At the time of his ordination, he was the Director of Nature Studies and Religious Education at the YMCA of the Rockies in Estes Park, Colorado.[97]

Karen Shipley Langlais became a Phoebe of Wyatt Park Christian Church in 1997, and *Anne-Nicole Walters* was added to the list of Phoebe's of Wyatt Park in 2008. At the time, she was serving full-time on the mission field in southwestern India. She currently serves as the full-time Worship Director at Eagle Mountain Fellowship, a non-denominational church in Bend, Oregon.[98] *Annetta Heckman* was recognized as a Phoebe of Wyatt Park Christian Church in January 2015.[99] Since early 2015, she has served on the mission field full-time on the island of Mindanao in the southern Philippines.

GOING FORWARD

As this is written (in 2017), at least two young adults at Wyatt Park are considering ministry as a possible vocation. Regardless of whether or not they

---

94 *The Call to Worship*, April 24, 1963.
95 *The Call to Worship*, September 12, 1968.
96 *The Call to Worship*, June 24, 1971.
97 *The Call to Worship*, January 31, 1974.
98 Board minutes, April 21, 2008.
99 Board minutes, January 20, 2015.

ultimately serve the church of Jesus Christ in that way, there will always be a call from God to His people: "Whom shall I send, and who will go for us?" (Isa. 6:8). Throughout its history, men and women from Wyatt Park Christian Church have arisen and said with the prophet, "Here I am! Send me" (Isa. 6:8). May it remain so as the twenty-first century continues to unfold.

———

And whatever you do, in word and deed,
do everything in the name of the Lord Jesus. (Col. 3:17)

WYATT PARK CHRISTIAN CHURCH IS (1) over 125 years old, (2) affiliated with
a mainline denomination, (3) located in an older residential area, and (4) in
a city with a population that changes little from decade to decade. Church-
growth experts would consider any one of those factors to be a strike against
the congregation in terms of prospects for the future. Those strikes are real,
but they do not tell the whole story or include factors that offer hope.

As I did research for this project, a clergy colleague asked if I had discovered any ingredients of Wyatt Park's DNA, essential elements at the heart of
the congregation's life and identity. It was a great question, and I have kept it
in mind since then. Now, after four years of research and nearly one year of
writing, I have identified four elements of Wyatt Park's DNA that give reason
for hope.

First, the congregation is willing to adapt to changing circumstances.
Whether with the facility, or programming, scheduling, organizational structure, or even worship style, throughout the congregation's history, there has
been a willingness to change when needed. Not that the changes were always
made easily or without resistance, but they have been made. Recent facility renovations and adjustments to educational offerings demonstrate a continuing willingness to adapt to changing circumstances. Such flexibility is

essential if the congregation is to make and grow disciples of Jesus in the twenty-first century.

Second, Wyatt Park Christian Church looks outward and has done so throughout its history. Over time, organizations often tend to turn inward, losing sight of their mission and instead focusing on preservation of what they have and caring for their own. Turning inward has led many congregations into irreversible decline. In years gone by, when institutions of all kinds were highly regarded, institutional preservation might have been a worthwhile goal, but not anymore. As the twenty-first century unfolds, most people seeking a church home look for congregations that look beyond themselves. They want to be part of a community of faith that has a positive impact not just on church members but also on local communities and beyond. Wyatt Park's consistent willingness to look beyond itself will serve it well in the years to come.

Third, a deep and genuine loving spirit is present. "Family church" is often how the congregation is described—and with good reason. Wyatt Park folk enjoy being together, so laughter is often heard. A genuine desire to love and care for one another is lived out in a variety of ways and at most any time, but it especially comes through when there is a serious challenge. From the pain of world wars and the Great Depression to the departure of the New Generation Singers and the theft of thousands of dollars by a former Business Manager, the people of Wyatt Park have loved one another through difficult times. Of course, there have been moments of anger when hurtful words were spoken and divisions were apparent, but anger and division did not have the final word. In an era when people often feel isolated and disconnected, a faith community that has a deep, genuine, loving spirit is both desirable and sought after. Wyatt Park Christian Church is positioned well in that regard.

Fourth, Wyatt Park Christian Church is deeply rooted at Twenty-Seventh and Mitchell, its home since 1928. Interestingly, in August 1928, the board considered a proposal to change the church's name. Board minutes do not specify how the name might have been changed, just that a name change was considered. The idea was brought up again that September, tabled, and then never brought up again. Although available documents do not indicate such conversations, it is likely that during decision making about large investments in the facility, there have been informal discussions about whether the congregation should move to a new location. It remains at 2623 Mitchell Avenue and, as of this writing, has a renewed commitment to connect more strongly with its neighbors. The ratio of rental homes to owner-occupied houses in nearby neighborhoods has changed over the years, but all of the houses are occupied by people who are loved by God and would be blessed to know Jesus Christ as Savior and Lord.

Finally, Wyatt Park's future is promising because its ultimate hope is in Jesus. I can think of no better words with which to conclude this congregational portrait than these words from the apostle Paul to the Colossians:

> Let the peace of Christ rule in your hearts, to which indeed you were called in one body. And be thankful. Let the word of Christ dwell in you richly, teaching and admonishing one another in all wisdom, singing psalms and hymns and spiritual songs, with thankfulness in your hearts to God. And whatever you do, in word or deed, do everything in the name of the Lord Jesus, giving thanks to God the Father through him. (Col. 3:15–17)
> Amen.

Alleluia.

ABOUT THE AUTHOR

DR. SCOTT KILLGORE JOINED THE Wyatt Park  Christian Church ministry staff as Associate Pastor in June 1996. He served in that capacity until January 2006, when he began his service as Senior Pastor, the position he still holds today. A native of northwest Missouri, he came to Wyatt Park after a seventeen-year career in broadcast journalism and then four years of seminary study. He holds a Master of Divinity from Lexington Theological Seminary in Lexington, Kentucky, and a Doctor of Ministry from Fuller Theological Seminary in Pasadena, California. He and his wife, Deirdra (Deedie), have three grown children.